The Bangor Dyslexia Teaching System

The Bangor Dyslexia Teaching System

Second edition

by

Elaine Miles

with the help of

Ann Cooke
Eileen Stirling
Judith Waddon
Anne Henderson
Felicity Roche
Eleanor Thomas

Dyslexia Unit,
University College of North Wales,
Bangor

Whurr Publishers
London

Whurr Publishers Limited
19b Compton Terrace
London N1 2UN
England

First published 1989
Second edition 1992
Reprinted 1993

**British Library Cataloguing in Publication
Data**
A catalogue record for this book is
available from the British Library

ISBN 1-870332-59-8

All royalties from this book will go to the
Dyslexia Unit, University College of North
Wales, Bangor

Typeset by Maggie Spooner, Typesetting,
London
Corrections and additions to the second
edition by Scribe Design, Gillingham, Kent
Printed in the UK by Athenaeum Press,
Newcastle upon Tyne

Preface

This is a programme for teaching dyslexic children, not just a reference book; but it is one which deliberately gives some choice to the teacher in planning the order of patterns taught, and some guidance on the principles of the spelling system, some of which he or she will be able to convey to the pupils.

The Bangor Dyslexia Teaching System is divided into two parts. The teaching material in Part I was originally produced in 1978 in order to give detailed guidance to the special team of teachers at the Dyslexia Unit, University College of North Wales, Bangor.

More recently, the material in this and Part II has been given to teachers from a wider area who attend MEd and Certificate of Further Professional Studies In-service courses at this college which specialise in the teaching of children who are dyslexic/have specific learning difficulties (we use these terms interchangeably).

In preparing both parts for publication extra material has been added on principles of teaching and teaching techniques, to make the book more suitable for teachers or speech and language therapists who are involved in teaching dyslexic children.

Part I is mainly intended for the teaching of primary school age children in order to bring them up to the standards of literacy, both in reading and written work, that are required for functioning up to their general ability level at secondary school. It is very important to remedy fundamental weaknesses as early as possible, certainly from 7 years of age, so that the children do not miss important parts of primary school education and get behind their peers. However, where there are cases of secondary school children who have similar literacy levels — and sadly these still exist at present — it will still be necessary for the teacher to go over the same ground; and he or she will have to do so systematically, picking out any points which cause difficulty and making clear the total structure of the spelling system so that these points are seen in relation to a framework. For this purpose words have been included in the lists, in brackets, which are suitable vocabulary for this age range rather than for the younger child. However, general advice on how to tackle the scattered nature of the older child's spelling faults will be reserved for Part II.

Part II is intended for secondary school pupils. Here too the teacher is expected to teach a structured systematic programme, and detailed advice on how to plan this, which seems initially a difficult task, is given in the Introduction to this second part. It is explained how to adapt the basic work of Part I and combine some of the material suitable for older children of which full resources are supplied in the rest of Part II for the teacher to select according to need. Contributions on essay writing and examination skills are also included.

I am grateful to all the teachers mentioned on the title page for their comments, and especially to Ann Cooke, Eileen Stirling and Judith Waddon for contributions to Part II. To Ann Cooke I owe an especial debt for generously giving help in the revision work over many years.

Finally, my thanks to my husband, Tim Miles, who was, or course, the originator of all our work and this 'dictionary'-centred method of working with dyslexics, and who has encouraged us all ever since.

In this, the second edition, not only has the material been updated, a task for which I owe a debt of gratitude to Ann Cooke and Dorothy Gilroy for their help, but also the introductions to Parts I and II and the early pages of Part I, Section 1 have been greatly expanded in response to requests for greater clarification as to how the programme is to be applied. Readers will find more detailed practical advice in the companion book *Tackling Dyslexia: The Bangor Way* by Ann Cooke, which will be produced by Whurr Publishers in the near future.

Elaine Miles, Dyslexia Unit
University College of North Wales, Bangor

Notation Used in Parts I and II

Written letters (graphemes) are in italics throughout. *Sounds (phonemes)* are enclosed in slanting brackets, e.g. /k/, in the symbols of the International Phonetic Alphabet. Approximate representations are given in brackets where necessary for teachers who, unlike speech and language therapists, do not necessarily know these symbols; a list of the phonetic symbols is to be found at the end of Part II. *Sample words* are enclosed in inverted commas. *Words in brackets in lists* are optional, either because they are more suitable for older children or occasionally because, although not having exactly the same sound as the others on the list, they follow naturally for teaching purposes, having the same root as the word just given (e.g. 'backwards', 'forwards', 'afterwards' can easily be taught after 'towards'). *Letters in brackets* are silent letters.

Contents

Part I

Introduction

Methods of teaching

Those who have tried to teach dyslexic individuals to read and write have always found that in order to obtain success they needed to concentrate on the alphabetic code, whether or not they called their approach a 'phonic' one. Many researchers[1] have confirmed in experimental work that intelligent children who fail at a fundamental level to acquire literacy skills experience difficulties with tasks of a phonological nature — that is to say with the 'handling' of sounds. This has aptly been termed 'phoneme deafness' rather than 'word blindness' by Uta Frith[2]. In all the different stages of learning to read and write, it is when learning the alphabetic code in particular, she considers, that dyslexics have trouble. Some young children have been found to have particular difficulty in sorting words by sound at the pre-reading stage; it has been shown[3] that such difficulties are an important factor in their subsequent failure to progress in the early stages of learning to read and spell.

Unless they have acquired, early on, a basic competence in recognising and categorising speech sounds children cannot go on to the more sophisticated approach to reading recommended by Frank Smith[4]. Nor can they learn to express themselves intelligibly on paper (a need that Smith and others of his school choose to ignore); spelling cannot be learned without the child looking closely at words, whether it slows down his reading or not, and the foundations of spelling cannot be laid by a solely visual methodology. Dyslexics have also often been found to score low on tests in which a good short-term or working memory is required, e.g. an auditory sequential memory test (digit span), and similarly have difficulty in learning and reciting multiplication tables. Working memory stores items phonetically, even sometimes items perceived visually, and such weaknesses could be the result of the phonological deficiencies mentioned above. However, there are phonological tasks, such as blending phonemes into a word, where short-term memory is clearly needed as a basis; thus it is not altogether certain how these two weaknesses are related. However, pupils having their own book to consult, filled in by them, in a way meaningful to them and involving understanding at the time, rather than mere rote learning, is helpful because in this way their intelligence is engaged.

In recent years research has been reported on ocular–motor problems, particularly the failure to acquire vergence early, which seems to be slightly more common in dyslexics than in good readers, and there have been claims of excessive sensitivity to dazzle being characteristic of a few cases. The possibility of any such weaknesses, which would not be spotted in ordinary basic eye tests, needs to be investigated if there is any doubt, for it seems that children progress in reading by picking out visual letter patterns, and the eyes certainly need to be efficient at their job to identify these correctly. More recently still, evidence has been reported of impairment in sensitivity of the 'transient' visual system, which analyses visual motion, in quite a large proportion of dyslexics. A number of these possible visual impairments are discussed by John Stein in a recent paper[5]. All this suggests that such aspects also need to be given more serious attention than was earlier thought. As well as the ability to pick up visual patterns, however, a child needs to acquire phonological skills in order to appreciate the function of such patterns in relation to speech and thereby to lay a foundation for spelling, and it is this need that the *Bangor Dyslexia Teaching System* programme is designed to meet.

Dyslexics can be and are being taught to read and write at a level where they can fully use their other abilities. But to achieve this level they have to learn the sound system of written language in a systematic way. This needs to be taught within a structure and the teacher has to proceed in a carefully ordered sequence of small steps, with plenty of cumulative and thorough revision and over-learning. They will then learn to use phonic cues automatically for reading, wherever needed, along with context cues, while in writing they will be able to communicate intelligibly and fluently, even if their spelling is not perfect.

Multisensory teaching

Basic literacy skills involve input from all the senses, plus the contribution of the mind in interpreting this sensory information. The linkages between written symbols (graphemes) and spoken sounds (phonemes) must be taught explicitly, and these are best learnt by engaging all the senses simultaneously, and also by ensuring that there is understanding. When children are given an auditory task, they should be provided with visual aids, and vice versa, and writing should go alongside reading whenever possible. At the same time the work should make sense, and never slide into mere rote learning; throughout, the pupil must be engaged in meaningful activity.

There are various ways of making the learning multisensory, and the teacher is strongly advised to use all of them, e.g.

1. Have cards to hand when teaching the grapheme/phoneme links. (These may be *Alpha to Omega* cards or Hickey cards or the letters of the *Edith Norrie Letter Case*, or others; see Materials list on pp. 41–42. The cards can also be used for drills to help the child to memorise them.

2. Give the child an exercise book or file in which to record all the spelling patterns as he learns them, with examples; this he will index and keep clear of clutter from practice work, so that he can use it for reference himself.

3. Dictate sentences in another book which practise the pattern being learnt, get the child to repeat them back, and then dictate them again slowly for him to write down. He can also be asked to read them back after writing, especially in order to pick out for himself any mistake that he has made. These sentences should not include any words containing patterns not yet learnt, nor any considered to have been learnt by sight, except possibly very basic ones like 'a', 'the', 'to', provided they are well known to the child. Examples of such sentences are given in the early pages of Part I. Subsequently recourse can be made to *Help for Dyslexic Children* and other books (see the list of Books and Materials on pp. 41–42. If this practice is observed the teacher will be able to insist on a very high standard of accuracy and never have to bypass errors. Every effort must be made to make the sentences both meaningful and as enjoyable as possible for the pupil, by relating them to his own particular interests and needs.

4. Use workbooks and exercises for practice (including any on the computer) which cannot be done *purely visually* but require the pupil to say the whole word to himself and identify it as a known word. (See Materials list, pp. 41–42, for suggested workbooks.)

Making the learning secure

Much repetition will be necessary; it is always desirable to begin a lesson by revising whatever was learnt in the last lesson. However, the child should not be asked to repeat what was taught last time entirely from memory without cards or his book for reference. Ways have to be found to work on the same pattern again and again without boredom, by using many different types of multisensory materials, both published and handmade, including the many games now available. (However, time spent on games should be brief, and the games strictly relevant, because time is precious!)

Even then, progress will be slow at the beginning, until the pupil is accustomed to approaching words in this way. Each stage must be secure before the next is started; otherwise it will be necessary for the pupil to go back and relearn, which is always boring and discouraging. As has been said by a famous American teacher in this field, Margaret Rawson, 'Go as fast as you can and as slowly as you must.' The pupil must always be kept busy and working at a good pace, even if on the same pattern.

The emphasis is always to be on 'patterns' rather than 'rules'. The word 'rule' suggests the learning by heart of some formula prescribed by the teacher. Rote learning, however, is to be avoided; also for dyslexics the intricacies of English spelling cannot be summed up in a few sentences.

Yet it does seem as if there are one or two rules which express pervasive principles. For instance there is the 'c' and 'g' rule (although this does not fully apply to the Anglo-Saxon element of the language, in which 'g' is 'hard' in general). Similarly, 'When two vowels go walking, the first one does the talking' seems to reflect a certain tendency in English spelling, viz. that often the first vowel in a vowel digraph indicates the *sort* of sound, *oa* being a sort of 'o' sound, and *ai* being a sort of 'a' sound. However, this fact is by no means always so obvious as to be helpful, since e.g. *ou* is not immediately recognisable as a sort of 'o' sound, while some of the imported digraphs, e.g. *ie* as in 'field', do not fit into that system at all. Consequently to memorise that as a 'rule' beyond the infant stage is not very useful.

Mnemonics make no pretence of embodying any principles. A few may occasionally serve to help the pupil to recall odd points, e.g.

> The cat catches.
> It itches.
> Ed on the edge.
> A piece of pie.

The pupil needs to be involved and doing, not just a passive listener, if he is to remember. *His* reference book, *his* examples, *his* choice of colours for highlighting and pictures for illustrations, *his* writing in the book all help to impress the work on his memory and provide props to recall it.

Reading

To obtain the most rapid progress possible, the teacher should avoid treating reading and spelling as separate topics, particularly at first, and rather teach them together so that they help each other on. This involves giving particular attention to the decoding aspect of reading and treating written work as something which will be read back when completed. Conversely, reading should also be used to help the written work, particularly in the early stages. Reading cannot therefore be left *exclusively* to supervision by parents or the child's other teachers, who cannot use it to reinforce the written work being done at the time. However, activities such as 'paired reading' with parents or older children, which encourage the child to take responsibility for deciding when he needs help, yet provides positive support, have much value as backup. Even with a teacher, reading should be a shared activity; the teacher can take a turn with the

reading, demonstrate enthusiasm for the book, serve as a model and keep the pace of the story going.

At a fundamental level, for a period of, say, six months, strictly phonic readers have much to commend them. They make clear, in a straightforward way, how grapheme and phoneme correspond to each other; and it is possible for the pupil to read them fluently and meaningfully, not sounding words out letter by letter, but nevertheless using the grapheme information all the time, so that it becomes a habit to use this information rather than to ignore it.

Oral language

Dyslexic children are not good at using oral language to plan their work. They need to be encouraged to try out words aloud, to respond aloud to cards, to state what exactly they have to do when executing a letter or when adding an ending to a word, and to say a sentence orally before writing it down. This is needed in order that later such verbalisation will turn into clear thinking and planning before action. Pupils need to be involved and to be active in making oral contributions to the lesson.

Notes and references

(1) For sources see in particular: (a) Isabelle Y. Liberman (1985), 'Should so-called modality preferences determine the nature of instruction for children with reading disabilities?' In F.H. Duffy and N. Geschwind (eds.), *Dyslexia: A Neuroscientific Approach to Clinical Evaluation*. Boston: Little, Brown and Co. (b) Margaret Snowling (1987), *Dyslexia: A cognitive developmental perspective*. Oxford: Blackwell.

(2) Uta Frith, at a conference of the Rodin Remediation Academy in Cambridge, 1986. For her discussion of such a phonological dysfunction see her chapter in K. Patterson, M. Coltheart, J.C. Marshall (eds.) (1985), *Surface Dyslexia*. London: Routledge and Kegan Paul.

(3) P.E. Bryant and L. Bradley (1985), *Children's Reading Problems*. Oxford: Blackwell.

(4) F. Smith (1971) *Understanding Reading*. New York: Holt, Rinehart & Winston.

(5) J.F. Stein (1991), 'Vision and language'. In M. Snowling and M. Thomson (eds.) *Dyslexia: Integrating Theory and Practice*. London: Whurr.

Plan of Part I

Part I is organised in six sections:

The first is concerned with single-letter sounds and the structure of single-syllable words, and therefore necessarily revolves round words containing 'short' vowels and the spelling practices associated with them. It is not envisaged that the teacher will teach all the less regular types of single-vowel word before moving on to the second section, but they are included here for easy reference and for use with older children who need to use them.

ar, or, er are to be found at the end of this section.

The second shifts to the commonest long vowel patterns, including the final *e* pattern, vowel digraphs, and combinations of a vowel and *w* or *y* serving a similar function.

The third supplies a basic checklist of irregular words which will be taught gradually, with suggestions on how to try to group them.

The fourth continues from Section 2 with more patterns (e.g. *ight, ir, ur*) and some less regular ones involving silent consonants (e.g. *ought, aught* and *ough*).

The fifth deals with silent consonant patterns and with the less common sound correspondences of some two-consonant combinations (e.g. *wh, ch* = /k/, *ch* = /ʃ/ (sh) etc.)

The sixth is concerned with word endings, including common grammatical endings (morphemes), and the changes to base words that sometimes have to be made when these are added.

Section 1

a e i o u   **y**

b c d f g h j k l m n p qᵘ r s t v w x y z

| sh | th | ch | wh | qu | | ph |

bl cr tw etc.

-ng
-nk

Basic Letter Sounds and the Structure of Words

Pupil's book

The book that the pupil is going to build up is central to the Bangor system of teaching. This is going to be his resource and reference book which he can take back with him to the classroom and have to hand when he is doing homework. It is *his* book, not one for the teacher to fill in and keep for him (although sometimes this becomes unavoidable in cases of constant forgetfulness!). It must therefore be laid out simply, with not too many examples of each spelling pattern and all of the words ones that he himself will want to use and that are familiar to him; expanding vocabulary is a different exercise altogether. The pages of the book will be highlighted by coloured pens and the pupil's own drawings which will act as a mnemonic, and the pupil will in due course make an index to enable himself to find his way around it, and to look up past patterns that have cropped up again and again in the lesson or need revision.

The inside cover of the book will look something like the page opposite, which is a record of the first task to be accomplished, that is mastering all the most usual sounds of single letters, then consonant digraphs and consonant blends. It is filled in gradually as the work proceeds. It may well not include *ph* or even *y* as a vowel until later. Each 'page' thereafter will represent a new pattern, although in fact sometimes several sheets will have to be allotted, e.g. for the whole topic of short vowels, some of them possibly being filled in later when that topic is being reviewed and there is the opportunity to add something.

What this book will be called may vary with the age of the pupil. The word 'Dictionary' represents its function well, even if this particular dictionary is not alphabetical! A file is considered more grown-up these days, and can be divided into sections with coloured dividers. It tends not to seem so personal and has a less permanent structure. (How does one index a file successfully?) A hard-backed exercise book or a gaudy-coloured semi-soft one might be more user-friendly for the primary school child. For the very young the delightful name 'Take-a-Look Book' was suggested to me by a Clwyd teacher; her pupil also had a 'Have-a-Go' book for practice work.

Very young children will probably not be ready to start the book straight away, being limited by their lack of handwriting skill. They will do better to start with a considerable period of word-building with plastic or cardboard letters, changing one letter to make a new word and so on, and learning the necessity of always keeping a vowel in the middle. Meanwhile they can be acquiring handwriting skills. Most younger children need word-building as a basis for starting the book, because words have a structure, not noticeable in written words on a page. Unfortunately most commercial plastic letters are coloured in a random way, but see Materials list (p. 41).

Begin by checking that your pupil knows the most usual sounds of *all the consonants*, including *y, qu* (rather than q), and the hard sounds of *c* and *g*. Simply write them all down, one by one, and ask for the sound. If given the *name* note it, but say 'That's the name; now I want the sound.' (Knowledge of names can be optional at this stage, but the teacher can use them.) When digraphs are introduced, names must be known, since the sound of *th* is not /t/ /h/ and the sound of *ai* is not /æ/ /ɪ/ . Check the consonant sounds until all are secure, but start building words with a few consonants and any short vowel known.

Teach five short vowels gradually. A good order is *a i o u e*. Teach how to mark the short vowel ŏ. Exclude *y* as a vowel at present, as it is rare in the middle of single-syllable words, being usually found in that position only in words of Greek origin (e.g. 'myth').

Record all these letters inside the front cover of the exercise book, building the page up gradually (see opposite).

Build words of three letters with short vowels. Make clear how words are constructed by putting the vowels down the middle and drawing up consonants on either side, or when writing use a coloured felt pen for the vowel. Make clear, as you go along, that this structure is to be found in all words, 'regular' or 'irregular'; irregular words can be analysed into consonants and vowels too, and irregularity of the pattern is a matter of degree.

e.g.   **cat**   **lau**g**h**
         ga**me**
         crea**m**

First page — short vowels

Once he is familiar with the consonants and short
vowels the pupil will start writing down words in his book
in five columns, headed by the short vowels. His first
words will all contain the same vowel, and so go in the
same column. Later the words will be mixed, so that he
has to think about the vowel in the middle before writing.
They will be dictated to him, and he should be able to
write them down without error, and equally to read them
back 'in one' without sounding the letters separately,
before proceeding further. If there is any difficulty over
this, he could initially sound them out under his breath
but later be asked to look carefully at them, without
making a sound, and produce the whole word. Phonic
readers give good practice in reading whole sentences
with meaning, even when the words are restricted to
those with short vowels in them plus 'a' and 'the' (see
Books and Materials list, p. 41). Whole sentences can
also be dictated for practice, on the same pattern, e.g.

> The cat bit the dog.
> Tom and Meg had a pet rat.

The pupil should repeat the sentence and assimilate
it, then have it dictated again, more slowly, to write
down. More sentences of this type are available in *Help
for Dyslexic Children* (see Book list, p. 41).

Words with single vowels should be included only if
the vowel is unmistakably short.

In some dialects /ʊ/ is the pronunciation for all u
words, and e.g. 'put', 'push', 'pull' etc., can be included.

Consonant digraphs and consonant blends

1. *Consonant digraphs* (*th*, *sh*, *ch*); add *wh* for the word
'when' and include *qu*. These combinations function as

extra letters of the alphabet — and indeed combinations
such as these are learnt as part of the Welsh alphabet.
Sample sentences for practice:

> Chop that log, Dad!
> The man shut the hen in the shed.

2. *Consonant blends*. These need gradual teaching, over
a longer period, since dyslexics are inclined to omit one
of two consonants blended together. Three consonants
must also be practised (e.g. *spl*), and digraph and blend
(e.g. *thr*), and blends at the end of a word as well as at
the beginning.
3. *-ng, -nk*. These combinations are associated with
short vowels. (Perhaps that is why 'young', the
exception, is pronounced with a short vowel.) Sample
sentences for practice:

> Jim must thank him.
> That song is a hit.

As the pronunciation of these combinations is
distinctive, they have to be studied specifically. Once
-ng is mastered it is possible to add the ending *-ing* to
verbs as long as this does not involve a doubling rule
which has not yet been taught. (The most suitable verbs
to use at this stage would be those which already end
in two consonants.) If a teacher wants to add *-ed*, see
p. 37 first.
4. *-ll, -ff, -ss, -ck, -tch*, and *-dge* endings. The use of
additional consonants is a feature of short-vowel words
of one syllable such as we are studying in this section,
and they come under the heading of 'doubling', to which
the teacher should now refer (see pp. 12–13). It may be
desirable to leave *-dge* until the soft *g* before an *e* has
been explained; this will be when final *e* pattern is
taught. However, the words should then be added to the
short-vowel lists, and the teaching of them included in a
session of revision on short-vowel words.

Note that when there is a consonant before one of
these endings, there is no doubling, even with a short
vowel, e.g.

> shelf   desk   bench   hinge

Sample first page (short vowels)

a	e	i	o	u
/æ/	/ɛ/	/ɪ/	/ɒ/	/uː/
cat	hen	pig	dog	pup
bat	ten	wig	log	cup
man	get	lid	box	rug
bag	bed	tin	top	fun
that	when	fish	chop	shut
clap	blend	crisp	frog	grunt
scrap		split		strut
bang	—	sing	long	hung
tank		pink	honk	sunk

Sample sentences for practice:

He fell off the cliff.
The clock is back on the shelf.
Jack will catch the logs and drop them in the sack.
The sledge went to the left and shot off the bridge.

Silly sentence: 'I shall be cross and cuff Jack if I catch him in the fridge.'

Sample first page entries (probably requiring a new sheet in the book)

shall	bell	hill	doll	gull
(staff)	—	cliff	off	cuff
mass	cress	hiss	loss	fuss
back	peck	lick	clock	stuck
match	fetch	stitch	Scotch	Dutch
badge	ledge	fridge	dodge	smudge

Most words in -all do not have short vowels; for these words see p. 15. In some regions the word 'staff' does, in others it does not.

Letter confusions

It is often believed that dyslexic errors are predominantly due to confusion between letters similar in pattern but of different orientations, or consist of reversals of order, and are thus visual in character. In fact it has been shown* by several researchers that these are only some of the letter mistakes made. Dyslexics have inadequate mastery of the alphabetic code in general.

In remedying any confusions, the teacher needs to link articulation, sound and visual appearance. *The Edith Norrie Letter Case* (see Books and Materials list, p. 41)', which arranges consonants in groups, labial, dental and gutteral, is particularly useful for this, and has a small mirror to demonstrate lip, teeth and tongue positions.

However, confusions between p and b, p and q, and especially between b and d are the most persistent errors usually. The problem is not only visual, but a mixture of visual and auditory–vocal elements not clearly discriminated. /p/ and /b/ are both bilabial plosives, one voiceless, the other voiced. /b/ and /d/ are both plosives too, with somewhat close places of articulation, and articulation may not be very clear. There is also the factor that d is the only lower case letter with an upright where the upright is not the first part made when it is written; it is the odd one out. This can easily have been overlooked by a child struggling with all sorts of problems with letters, and he starts to write both b and d the same way. The upper case letters do not differ in this way; they have different patterns.

The objective in trying to remove the confusion is to *dis*associate the letters. It is therefore not helpful to

teach or practise them together or provide similar ways of remembering each of them. Although the well-known mnemonic *bed* is a possible final resort to settle doubt, it still keeps the letters linked together. It is often the case that pupils can tell the letters apart when they are together, but when they are reading or writing they normally need to identify one letter on its own.

It is probably useful to make a link for d with c, the preceding letter in the alphabet; after writing c, one starts in the same way for a d. On the other hand b can easily be remembered by a picture mnemonic, 'bat and ball', the upright being the bat.

Correct letter production as a basis for correct letter concept is very important (see Handwriting section on p. 40). When errors are made, even in reading, the pupil can be asked to go back to the letter production and trace the letter with his finger on the desk, and give the correct name. As often in teaching dyslexics, saying aloud what he has to do, e.g. 'start with c and turn it into d', gives multisensory reinforcement and also a directive to follow.

Doubling I

What follows is all that needs to be taught to young children at this stage, because they are dealing only with one-syllable words. The second section is concerned with longer words and some of it may be useful for some older children. It seems convenient to handle the whole subject here together.

When one-syllable words with short vowels in them end in the sounds /l/, /f/, /s/, /k/, /z/, /tʃ/ (ch), /dʒ/ (j), the letters representing those sounds are duplicated (or in the last two cases partly duplicated). Thus:

   -ll   -ff   -ss   -ck (not -kk)   -tch   -dge

In the last two cases, because the sound is already represented by two letters, only the first part of the sound is duplicated. If children try it out for themselves, they will find that t is the closest single letter in sound to /tʃ/ , and d to /dʒ/ . *chch* and *gege* would be just too

* For example Isabelle Liberman's research group counted 15% of reversals of letter orientation and 10% of transpositions out of the total of errors in a sample of writing from retarded readers of second grade age. The other 75% was made up of other consonants (32%) and other vowels (43%). (Liberman, I.Y., Shankweiler, D., Orlando, C., Harris, K., and Bell-Berti, F. *Cortex*, 1971, **7**, 127–142.)

clumsy! If they find these endings hard to remember they could try these mnemonics:

Don't Get Excited	-DGE
Try Concentrating Hard	-TCH

There are four exceptions which might be entered in the lists in colour:

which	such
rich	much

These have no *t*. Take care to indicate that 'which?' not 'witch' is meant.

There are also a few exceptions to the *ss* ending, mostly small grammatical words, e.g. 'his', 'has', 'is', 'this', 'thus', or abbreviations, e.g. 'gas', 'bus'.

There are a few other individual words which end in a double consonant, and this often serves to distinguish them from another word, e.g. inn/in, matt/mat, sett/set, and putt/put. In other cases, e.g. 'add', 'odd', 'egg', the addition of the extra letter gives them the status of a three-letter word; English nouns, verbs and adjectives are normally at least of this length.

Doubling II (polysyllables)

This second section need not be taught now. It is probably more suitable for a more advanced stage unless the pupil is a secondary school pupil.

The doubling of consonants occurs when there is a short vowel in a stressed syllable. A single consonant at the end of the syllable is usually doubled when the next syllable begins with a vowel, or a vowel *sound*, as in the *-le* combination. Otherwise the vowel tends to lengthen the preceding vowel, much as final *e* does. Doubling 'protects' the short vowel sound.

Compare the pronunciation of these pairs of words which have various second syllables, but all beginning with a vowel *or vowel sound* (*-le*).

Short vowel with double consonant	*Long vowel with single consonant*
hopping	hoping
fitted	sited

little	title
tripper	wiper
Jimmy	slimy
village	silage
supper	super

However, normally *v* is not doubled, e.g. 'river'.

This principle still holds with longer words whenever a *stressed* syllable has a short vowel.

Short vowel	*Long vowel*
tobŏggan	lōganberry
permĭtting	recītal

It should be noted that the vowel pronunciations of

ar	*or*	*er*	*ir*	*ur*

normally change when followed by a syllable beginning with a vowel to long vowel with single *r* or short vowel with double *r*. Compare:

mar	Mary	Harry
her		cherry
sir	wiry	mirror
for	story	lorry
cur	fury	hurry

But note: star — starry, fur – furry to preserve the meaning.

The doubling principle is not quite universally applied in English, because words have come into the language from other languages (particularly Greek) which do not have such a principle, and habitually have short vowels without two consonants following. Perhaps Greek, having a more even stress on syllables, did not suffer vowel change so readily.

The pupil will have to note these words as he comes across them. Here are some Greek patterns: words ending in

-ic, e.g. 'panic', 'tonic', 'clinic', 'topic', 'comic'
-ology, e.g. 'geology', 'chronology'
-el, e.g. 'camel', 'panel'

There are also a few words from other languages, e.g.

robin, damage, manage
finish, vanish, polish
rapid, solid, timid
city, very, body

It is pointless to try to apply the distinction between open and closed syllables to such words. (For this distinction see Part II, p. 50.

Plurals and hissing plurals

1. When one is practising the sound /ks/ with short vowel words it is often necessary to make clear the distinction between the use of the letter *x* and -*ks* or -*cks*, as follows:

tanks ⎫
⎬ more than one thing
clocks ⎭

box ⎫
⎬ one thing
fox ⎭

-*s* being an ending which indicates 'more than one'.

2. However, when adding this ending to words which end with complex combinations such as -*x*, -*ch*, -*ss*, -*s*, one finds that if *s* on its own is added the result is unpronounceable. A vowel therefore needs to be inserted and the ending is -*es*, e.g.

boxes
brushes
benches
pitches
crosses
buses

Likewise, of course,

hedges   (but in these cases there is an *e*
horses   already)

The extra syllable can be heard quite clearly.

Variations in the sound of single vowels

These variations are given next for the sake of logical arrangement, and because the teacher may want to include just a few common words, especially for older pupils.

Teachers may well want to teach 'w' words early, while they are dealing with short vowels, if the pupil can handle them.

In general, however, teachers are advised not to linger too long on single vowels to the exclusion of the other vowel patterns needed by pupils. They would do well to move on at this point to one out of three possibilities:

1. *ar, or, er* (pp. 15–16).
2. Final *e* pattern, making the contrast with short vowels (p. 18).
3. *oo, ee* — a pattern which may be familiar to young pupils (p. 20).

'w' words

Words with single vowels in them, but with *w* (or *qu*) before an *a* or *o*, normally have a different pronunciation from the usual short vowel sound. *qu* (originally *cw*) contains a /w/ sound and therefore has the same effect on the vowel.

wa- is pronounced /wɒ / (wŏ)
wo- is pronounced /wʌ / (wŭ)

Examples:
was, want, what, wash, watch, swan, squash, quality, quantity, etc.
won, wonder, wonderful, worry (but 'wolf' is odd)

In such words the vowel is still short and therefore still takes the short vowel endings:

-*ll*, -*ff*, -*ss*, -*ck*, -*tch*, and -*dge*
(e.g. 'watch' and 'quaff').

Note that in 'water' *wa* has a longer sound, where there is no double *t* to shorten it.

war- and wor- are also pronounced differently from the normal 'ar' and 'or', e.g.

war, warn, ward, warm, quart, quarter,
work, worm, worse, world, etc.

It has sometimes been suggested that the reason for writing *wo* for a 'wŭ' sound (and so *wa* for 'wŏ') is due to the similarity, in mediaeval manuscript, of letters like *w*, *u*, *n* and *m*. The same reason is given for *o* being written for the short 'u' sound with *m* and *n* in *come*, *done*, etc.

Alternatively, as in the case of the letter *l*, the articulation of a *w* may be more easy with some vowel sounds than with others, and this may have caused changes in pronunciation.

'l' words

Words with a single vowel in them, but with an 'l' immediately after it, also have unusual pronunciations of the vowels, and sometimes the 'l' is not heard at all, e.g.

> all, wall, hall, etc.
> old, cold, hold, etc.
> talk, walk, chalk, stalk,
> salt, halt
>
> (bald, palm, calf, yolk, roll, bull,
> scald, calm, half, folk , poll, pull, etc.)*

A similar effect is found in the following words with *two* vowels:

> could, would, should

It is usually desirable to omit 'w' and 'l' words for the time being and move on to vowel digraphs, which are more familiar, especially to a young child. One can, however, leave a page, or start a page which is completed later.

* Where words are placed in brackets the intention is that they should be taught later, since they are likely to be too advanced for the pupil's present stage.

Long single vowels

mind	wild	most	both	truth
find	child	post		
behind	mild		com(b)	
etc.				

Broader 'a' (stays short in northern dialects)

pass	bath	ask	father	last
glass	path	task	rather	mast etc.
		mask		

'o' for 'u' (see Basic irregular word checklist, p. 24)

son	other	come	one
among	another	some	done
front	mother	(company	money
sponge	brother	comfort	love
	nothing	compass)	glove
			above etc.

Many such words have 'n', 'm', 'v' or 'th' after the 'o'.

ar, or, er

There are a number of simple common words containing *ar* and *or*, and these are quite straightforward, e.g.

car	horn
farm	form
cart	fort
yard	pork

It is probably a good moment to introduce 'are', which has a silent *e* on the end. It is usual for 'or' words to end in *-ore* and only the three function words 'or', 'nor' and 'for' are found with *-or* alone. (The two common words, 'door' and 'floor', can be learned individually at this point as irregular words.)

er is most common as an ending, e.g. 'wait*er*', and this should be stressed, as later the pupil will meet words containing *ir* and *ur* which in fact are used to spell that sound medially in one-syllable words much more frequently, than *er*. A few common words are worth including which have an *-er* medially, e.g.

her(s)	nerve
term	serve
herd	swerve

The last three introduce *-ve* endings. English words do not end in *v*. 'were', with a silent *e*, can also be introduced in the same way as 'are'.

Section 2

Long Vowels

A single vowel at the end of a word or syllable is normally long, e.g.

a	me	I	no	(g)nu
	we		go	
	the			
			tomato	
sha-ken	pre-tend	pi-lot	pro-tect	tu-lip

The sound is the same as the name of the letter, except that the sound of long *u* can be either /u/ or /ju/(yoo). The long vowel can be marked ‾, e.g. ō. 'a' and 'the' are pronounced with a schwa in normal speech, unless emphatic and children should be discouraged from reading the word 'a' with a short or long vowel.

Otherwise a long vowel is usually expressed by two vowels, either together in a vowel digraph, or separately, as with the final *e* pattern, which will be studied next.

Final *e* pattern

The pattern is a very good logical choice after single vowels, because of the great contrasts in end-of-word patterns between the two, and the basis that this provides for doubling principles. It is useful, therefore, to have accompanying visual aids, e.g. concentric wheels, which can rapidly turn a short-vowel word, e.g. 'hat' into a long-vowel word, e.g. 'hate', to impress the differ-ence on the pupil. The fact that the two vowels of the pattern have to be abstracted from their intermediate consonant makes it a rather complex pattern, but it is better to think of it like this than to give any suggestion of going *back* from the e to the vowel to change the sound; that reading is from left to right is a principle that one wants to maintain.

This should be treated as one unit (vowel–con-sonant–e) since that is how it is read, and the headings should consist of the whole unit, e.g. *a-e*. Since *e-e* is rather rare, and much less common than the digraphs

ee and *ea* which represent the same sound, there is no need to put more than a few token words into that column at this stage.

The same can be said for *u–e*, which is less common than *oo*. Also the variation between /u/ and /ju/(yoo) can be puzzling.

It is important to spend time on the distinction between a short-vowel word, e.g. 'mat', and the long-vowel word produced by adding an *e* on the end — 'mate', e.g.

hat	hate
bit	bite
pet	Pete
not	note
cut	cute

The double endings learnt for short-vowel words do not occur when the word has a long vowel, and this means a contrast between, e.g.

Short vowel	Long vowel
back	bake
cadge	cage

Making these distinctions also needs practice.

Before using words ending in -*ce* or -*ge* the teacher will have to introduce the *c* and *g* rule, at least partially. (See p. 19 for this.)

Using words ending in -*re* (e.g. 'care', 'here', 'fire') brings a slight change in the vowel sound, so these words can be deferred, if the teacher wishes. They will be found on p. 29 when required.

c and *g* rule

This rule is very important for accurate word attack of new words. (Welsh children are unused to 'c' and 'g' having soft sounds.)

Sample second page (long vowels — final *e* pattern)

a – e	*e – e*	*i – e*	*o – e*	*u – e*
game	these	ride	bone	tune
cage	Pete	mice	note	rule
bake		(w)rite	rose	cube
		like		

The combinations also occur together at the end of a word in a few cases; *-ee* is especially common.

Together at the end

—	*-ee*	*-ie*	*-oe*	*-ue*
	see	die	toe	blue
	bee	tie	doe	glue
	tree	pie	hoe	due
	three etc.	lie		

The rule states:

1.   *c* + *e, i* or *y* is *soft* (/s/)
       g + *e, i* or *y* is *soft** (/dʒ/)

* This is *usually* so. There are a small number of common exceptions — get, give, girl, etc. — which are words of Saxon (i.e. German) origin. In German, like Welsh, *g* is always hard.

2.   c + a, o, u or a consonant is *hard* (/k/)
     g + a, o, u or a consonant is *hard* (/g/)

Examples:
Soft: cell, city, cycle
             gentle, giant, gym

Hard: cat, cot, cut, clap, crisps
             game, got, gull, glad, grass

It follows that:

1.   -*ge* is used as a /dʒ/ ending (since *j* is not found at the end of a word), e.g. 'hinge'.
2.   -*ce* is often used as a /s/ ending, e.g. 'prince'.
3.   *k* must be used for words like 'kettle' and 'king', although normally *c* is more common to start a word.
4.   It is necessary to use *j* for words like 'jam' and *job'*.
5.   When a hard sound is required for a *g* but *e* or *i* follows, a silent vowel is inserted, viz. *u*, which will make the *g* hard, e.g. 'guest', 'guide'.†
6.   When a soft sound is required but *a* or *o* follows, a silent *e* is inserted which will make it soft, e.g. 'George', 'pageant'.† (Note that the 'e' in this word is *not* lengthening the vowel.)

Vowel digraphs

Vowel digraphs are very numerous in English, and the best order of teaching them is determined by three factors:

1. Their frequency in children's early reading books.
2. Where the same sound has several different possible spellings they must be kept well apart as pupils are confused between the two.
3. The need to make links between natural pairs, like *ay* and *ai*.

The most common vowel digraphs are probably *oo, ee, oa, ou, ay, ea, ai*.

oo: There are two possible sounds to this digraph

     oo as in 'soon' /u/
     oo as in 'good' /ʊ/

It is confusing for dyslexics if these differences are glossed over and not pointed out.

ee: There is much possibility for confusion with *ea*, because both are used medially and finally. Here the teacher has to give thought to building up separate associations from *ea* by inventing links. A small number of words should be made secure, e.g.

queen	meet	street
see	seen	
green	trees	
beech	trees	
feed	sheep	geese

ea: Similar links can be made between, e.g.

seat	eat	meal	feast
peas	beans		
weak	tea		
cheap	meat		
peaches	cream		
sea	beach		

Silly pictures or sentences can help to establish these links. Story material in *Tall Stories* or phonic stories like those in *Primary Phonics* can help to link the words together in a story context (see Materials and Books list, p. 41).

oa: This digraph is found in the middle of words only, but confusion will arise with words containing the *o–e* pattern, and particularly between 'road' and 'rode', unless the 'ride–rode' link has been secured earlier when final *e* pattern was being taught.

---

† It is not necessary to teach this point at the first introduction of the rule.

Pairs

At some time in England it became the practice to use a y to denote an i at the end of a word, and a w to denote a u. This practice has produced pairs of vowel combinations to represent the same sound in final and medial positions respectively, e.g.

Finally	Medially
-ay	-ai-
-ey	-ei-
-oy	-oi-
-ow	-ou-
-aw	-au-
-ew	-eu-(rare)

The sounds of -ey and -ei meant here are those of -ey as in 'they', and -ei as in 'vein'.

The most important to teach first are -ay and -ai-, -ow and -ou-, and -oy and -oi-.

The allocation of -ou- to a medial and -ow to a final position is not quite so clearcut, since ow is found medially as well. However, there is a pattern of use of each in the medial position:

ow before:

n	l	el	er
down	howl	towel	flower (on plant)
	fowl (bird)	vowel	

ou before:

t	d	r	se	2 consonants
out	loud	flour (cake)	house	ground

There are a few exceptions, e.g. 'foul' (shot), 'crowd', 'browse'.

ow with a long 'o' (/aʊ/) sound has a similar pattern of use, likewise aw, before:

n	l	er
grown	bowl	mower
dawn	crawl	drawer

Other less common vowel combinations need to be left till later

ea   (/ɛ/ or /ei/) as in 'head', 'great'.
ie   (/i/) as in 'field'.
ei   (/i/) as in 'ceiling' — most often after c.
-ey   (/i/) as in 'key' and with a less definite sound in an unstressed syllable at the end of a word, e.g. 'donkey'.
-ey at the end of place names, e.g. 'Jersey', 'Anglesey', is from a Scandinavian word meaning 'island' (cf. 'eyot'/ 'ait').
ui   as in 'fruit'.

Section 3

Irregular Words

The commonest irregular words begin to be needed as soon as the first foundations of short and long vowels have been laid.

It is a good idea to have copies of a checklist which contains the most common ones. From the very beginning one can start ticking off words such as 'he' and 'she' as one observes that the pupil knows them. Below is a specimen checklist.

Even the irregular words should be taught in meaningful groups and with reference to principles, so that the pupil can see where they fit into the general framework. They should not be taught all at once, but gradually, group by group; they can then provide variety from the vowel digraphs.

In brackets the teacher will find indications as to how a particular word can be taught.

Basic irregular word checklist

Question words begin with wh, except: 'how'

when	which	what	why	where	(w)ho
	(no *t*)	(*wa*)	(-*y*)		(do)
					(to)

Some words have o when the sound is /ʌ /(ŭ)

mother	son	one	com(e)	lov(e)
brother	among	once	som(e)	glov(e)
other	front	none	(com-)	dov(e)
another	sponge	done		abov(e)

Other words, besides some of those above, have an e which is not affecting the sound

ar(e)	giv(e)	gon(e)
wer(e)	hav(e)	

Links can be made between:

go	do
goes	does
gone	done

The sound of a in these words varies in different regions, but in some areas it is almost like / ɑː / (ah)

father	bath	ask	last
rather	path	task	fast
			past

People and possessions

I	me	he	she	we	you	they
						(-*ey*)

my	mine	his	her(s)	our(s)	your(s)	their(s)
				(*ou*)	(*you+r*)	(-*ei*-)

Mr   (*M* iste *r* — first and last letters)
Mrs   (Mr + *s* — 'Mistress' has *s* on the end)

Place

h *ere*	th *ere*	wh *ere*

(All end with -*ere*, and all are 'place' words.)

Numbers

one	t(w)o	three	four
once		(*ee*)	(4 letters not 3)

Other groups

any	both	go	is
many	truth	no	was
	only	so	(*wa*)

close	touch	could	(I affects the
move	young	would	sound of the
prove		should	vowel)

-s is for plurals and third persons, so use -se in:

please   cause (au)   because

Days of the week

Monday (*o* for /ʌ /), Tuesday (*ue*), Wednesday
(pronounce as three syllables), Thursday (*ur*), Friday (*i* for
y in the middle), Saturday (*ur*)

Seasons

Spring   Summer   Autum(n) (*au*)   Winter

Months

month (*o* for /ʌ /) — attach them to seasons and learn
the order.
January, February, March, April, May, June, July (-*y*),
August (*au*), September, October, November, December.
We say 'br' in February!

Numbers

seven, eight (*ei*), eleven, twelve, thirteen (*ir*), fourteen,
fifteen, sixteen, twenty, thirty, forty, fifty, sixty, seventy,
eighty, ninety, a hundred, a thousand, a million (doubling).

Persons

brother, sister, a(u)nt, uncle, cousin,
nephew (*ew*), niece (like 'piece'), grandfather,
grandmother,
fr(i)end, people, woman, women.

Section 4

More Basic Patterns

-ight, -ought, -aught

ight	ought	aught
right (OK)	bought	caught
sight	brought	naughty
light (alight)	thought	daughter
fight	ought	taught
tight	fought	slaughter
night (and day)	nought	(haughty)
knight (on horseback)	(sought)	
bright		
might (strength)		
might (may)		

Silly sentences

I *bought* a football and *brought* it home.
I *thought* I *ought* to score a goal.
I *fought* hard but I still got *nought*.
I *caught* my *naughty daughter* and *taught* her not to *slaughter*.

It is useful to put all these words on cards for regular drills.

These difficult spellings have arisen because the words were originally Anglo–Saxon, with Saxon (German) guttural sounds in them. When a Latin alphabet came to be used for written English there was no equivalent to such sounds, and although the nearest *individual* letters were chosen, viz. *g* and *h*, such letters *in combination* were quite foreign to a Latin-based language; they remained in spelling but disappeared from the pronunciation like the silent letters on pp. 32–33. There are past tenses in both the *ought* and the *aught* lists, but it is useful to note that the two on the *aught* list ('caught' and 'taught') are from verbs which have an *a* in the present tense ('catch' and 'teach').

Notes

igh is also found without the *t*, as in *high*, *thigh*, *nigh*.

aught and *augh* are sometimes found with irregular *au* pronunciation, as in *laugh*, *laughter*, *draught*, where the sound is / ɑː /.

Other *-gh(t)* words with regular vowel sounds are: *straight*, *eight*, *weight*, *neigh*, *sleigh*.

height has borrowed an *e* by analogy with *weight* but kept the original vowel sound of *high*.

More 'r' combinations

(The teacher will have to select which of these to include for each pupil.)

er was included on p. 16. There are two other ways of spelling the same sound, which in fact are more frequent medially in one-syllable words:

ir			ur	
skirt	fir	first	fur (cat)	Thursday
shirt	(tree)	third	turn	Saturday
dirt	sir	thirteen	burn	
	girl	thirty	nurse	
	bird	birthday	purse	
			church	

wor is also pronounced in this way (see 'w' words, p. 14).

ear as in 'earth' is uncommon, but is also found in 'earn', 'learn', 'heard', 'early', 'search', 'earnest' (and 'year' is pronounced this way by some people).

-are, -ere, -ire, -ore, -ure

-ore has been mentioned already under *or* (p. 15). In the other final *-e* combinations the introduction of an *r* changes the long vowel sound slightly. Some of the words in the *are* list have homophones in *-air*, and here the more common homophone has been included in its list to become secure first. The less common one may therefore appear in its list in brackets.

-are	-ere	-ire	-ore	-ure
bare feet	here	fire	more	cure
care	sphere	wire	core	sure
dare	interfere	hire	store	pure
bus fare		tire (out)	tore	
welfare		spire	shore	
mare (horse)			wore (dress)	
share				
spare				
beware				
(stare)				

Same sound as -are

-air	-ear
fair hair	great bears
pair (2)	eat pears
repair	tear
stairs	wear
chair	

Same sound as -ere

-eer	-ear
deer (Bambi)	dear (£)
beer glass	fear
steer	gear
sheer	ear
queer	hear
	clear
near	spear
year	shears

-y, -ie

-y and -ie are virtually interchangeable, being pronounced like a long 'i' in stressed syllables (e.g. 'try', 'reply', 'die') and rather like a short 'i' in unstressed syllables ('happy', 'hurry', 'duties'). y came to be used as a way of writing an i at the end of a word.

There are only a limited number of words of one syllable ending in -y, e.g.

by	why	try	cry	fry	dry	pry
my	sky	sty	spy	shy	fly	ply

And there are only five common words which end in -ie:

pie
tie
die
lie (in bed)
lie (tell lies)

These five have only one consonant and would be two-letter words if spelled with -y. Since nouns and verbs in English normally have more than two letters, this could be the reason why -ie is used for these words.

Both types have -ie when an s is added, e.g. 'tries', 'duties', 'dies'.

The addition of y often gives a descriptive character, e.g. 'sticky', 'dusty', 'misty', 'rainy'.

For changes in -y/-ie when endings -ed, -ing are added, see p. 37.

When y is found in the middle of a word as a short vowel, the word is normally derived from Greek. Such words are few in number and can be learned individually. As with 'i', the addition of a final -e produces a long 'i' sound. y here is in origin the Greek upper case symbol for u. The Romans used it in Greek words to distinguish them from Latin words.

myth	type	physics	python
hymn	style	rhythm	pylon
gym	rhyme	cylinder	cycle
		mystery	nylon

(The word 'tyre' is not Greek, but perhaps the y serves to distinguish it from 'tire' = weary.)

-ough

It is better to keep these words separate from -ought. To put them together makes a group with too many variations to be readily memorable. Moreover, -ough, despite all its various sounds, never in fact overlaps in sound with -ought, whereas ought and aught do have the same sound. It therefore seems most helpful to differentiate them as much as possible from ought words by teaching them in a quite different way. One can make a chart with all the different pronunciations as headings. (If this is put longways on the page it makes a further difference to make them more memorable.)

o	oo	ou
dough	through	plough
though		bough
although		

off	*uff*	*urrer*
cough	rough	thorough
trough	tough	borough
Frank Bough	enough	

The lists can be read regularly until the words are very familiar. Spelling is little problem once the word is recognised as belonging to this list.

The words can be read first with the phonetic cues visible, then with them covered.

Section 5

Silent Letters and Other Two-letter Combinations

Some of these words are more appropriate for secondary school pupils, but it is more convenient to list them all together.

Silent letters at the beginning of words

One letter is silent in English in the following combinations at the beginning of words:

(k)n	(g)n	(w)r	(s)c
know	gnaw	write	scent
knew	gnome	wreck	scene
knight	gnat	wrong	sceptre
knit	gnash	wrap	sceptic
knot	gnu		science
knee		s(w)	scissors
knuckle	g(h)	sword	scythe
knife	ghost	answer	
	ghastly		
	ghetto		

These are mostly Saxon (German) combinations, fully pronounceable in the original language.

The combination (s)c presents no problem when the c is hard, but the sounds of the two letters merge before e, i or y.

In the following words, the first letter is silent in English. In the original Greek both were pronounced:

(p)n	(p)s	(p)t
pneumonia	psychology	pterodactyl
	psalm	

st in the middle of words

The t is silent sometimes in this combination.

castle	listen	bustle	jostle
bristle	fasten	hustle	apostle
thistle	glisten	rustle	
whistle	hasten		(w)restle
gristle			trestle
epistle			nestle

Silent letters at the end of words

The last letter is silent in the following combinations found at the end of words.

m(b)		m(n)	(b)t
crumb	plumber	hymn	debt
numb	(succumb)	Autumn	doubt
dumb		solemn	
thumb		column	
lamb		damn	
limb		condemn	
bomb			
climb			
comb			
tomb			
womb			

Originally these words had further letters on the end, which made the consonants more pronounceable; they are often pronounced in words which come from the same root but have a suffix added, e.g.

limber, autumnal, solemnity, hymnal.

Comparing these words reminds the pupil of the presence of the sometimes silent letters.

gn at the end of a word will be found in Part II.

Other two-letter combinations

wh

1. Question words usually begin with wh-, even if they do not all sound as if they do (e.g. who, whom, whose). The exception is how.

The *wh* gives a 'breathy' sound;* one is perhaps breathless with wonder as to what the answer will be!

2. Other *wh* words may have a 'breathy' sound inherent in the meaning of the word, in that they often denote a whispering noise or movement, e.g.

whistle	whet(stone)	wheeze
whine	whack	wheel
whizz	whimsy	whirr
whoa	whisk	whisper
		whirl

Two lovely phrases to remember are:

the whirring wheel
the whispering ears of wheat

If we remember that whales spout, that seems to leave only *white* and *while* without any explanation.

ch Greek /k/

school	Christ	anchor	stomach
choir	Christopher	chemistry	architect
chorus	Christmas	chemist	orchid
chord	ache	technical	character
chasm	echo	mechanical	chrome
chaos			

The original Greek letter was aspirated like Welsh *ch*. It was a *single* letter, which is represented by the consonant digraph *ch* in English.

ch (French) /ʃ/

machine	chassis
chute	creche
parachute	chalet
cache	chef
	champagne

Some of these words are too advanced at this stage, but they are listed together for convenient reference.

*The pronunciation of *wh* in a 'breathy' way, however, has largely fallen into disuse.

Section 6

Endings

There are some common word endings, which need discussion, viz.

-ed   -ve   -se   -ze   -ce   -le   -tion   -ture

-ed

This is a grammatical ending added on to a verb to denote the past tense. The whole *-ed* ending is to be written even if the *e* cannot be heard, as in 'called', or if the *d* sounds like a 't', as in 'hoped'. However, if the original verb ended in an *e*, the *e* of the *ed* is already there.

It may be that older children will like to know that there are a few cases where the past tense really does end in *t*. These are words in which the original word has undergone a change to the inner sound.

creep	crept
sleep	slept
mean	meant
dream	dreamt
hear	heard

It is interesting to note that the change of the inner sound in the last three does not involve a change of spelling of that sound, because *ea* can represent both sounds. Since *ee* cannot, there has to be a change to a single *e*.

A few past tenses are at a transitional stage. For instance there is both 'dreamt' and 'dreamed', 'learnt' and 'learned', 'burnt' and 'burned', and in the last two no change of sound has taken place.

-ve, -ze

No English word ends in *v* or *z* (unless doubled as in 'fizz'), so an *e* is added, without it necessarily also lengthening the preceding vowel, e.g.

'have' 'give' 'live'
'breeze' 'baize'

-se, -ce

Single *s* is used to indicate a plural or third person ending, as in 'ducks' or 'sings', the use of *-se* serves to make clear that the word is *not* plural or third person singular. Thus we have verbs ending in *-se*, e.g. 'raise', or nouns, e.g. 'horse'.

-le

The sound of this ending is / ᵊl /. The spelling is *-le* more often than *-el*, since it is normally only after soft consonants such as *w*, *r*, *s*, etc., that *-el* is preferred. The *-el* ending can therefore be learned later, as can the adjectival *-al* ending, which will not be met so often by younger children.

It can be explained even to young pupils that it is necessary to put *e* after soft *c* and soft *g*, since this follows from a rule already learned, e.g.

parcel
angel

Note: in *-stle* combinations the *t* is silent, but the spelling is still *-le* rather than *-el*.

-tion, -ture /ʃə/   /tʃə/

The sounds of these endings are approximately 'shun' and 'cher'.

Words should be practised with both these endings.

There are *some* words, however, which are spelled '-cher'. These are words which add *-er* to a base word ending in *-ch*, as in:

teacher   catcher   poacher

In contrast, the *-ture* words would be incomplete if the endings were taken away, as can be seen from the following examples:

pic – ture   lec – ture   na – ture

Rules for adding grammatical endings

1. No changes are needed before a grammatical ending in the case of words

> which end in two
> consonants   e.g. 'bank' 'fish'
> which end in vowel + *y*   e.g. 'play', 'enjoy'
> which end in vowel + *w*   e.g. 'snow'
> which have two vowels
> before a single consonant e.g. 'heat'

Examples:

> 'fishing'   'played'   'snowy'   'heater'

However, a few *-ay* words show irregularities

pay	paid	
lay	laid	
say	said	
day	daily	
gay	gaily	gaiety

2. Words ending in *e* usually drop the *e*, whatever function that *e* has been serving, before an ending beginning with a vowel.

Examples with *-ing*:

hate	hating	(*e* lengthening vowel)
mince	mincing	(*e* softening *c*)
cage	caging	(*e* softening *g*)
raise	raising	(*e* of *-se* termination)
leave	leaving	(*e* of *-ve* termination)

However, when *e* is softening *c* or *g*, and the ending begins with *a*, *o* or *u*, the *e* is retained; but these involve more advanced endings than are likely to be met at this stage, e.g. 'irreplaceable', 'curvaceous', 'manageable', 'gorgeous'.

'singeing' keeps its *e*. This differentiates it from 'singing'. (Note that 'fringing' and 'hinging' drop the *e*.)

'dyeing' keeps its *e*. That differentiates it from 'dying'.

3. Words ending in a single consonant after a single short vowel have to double the consonant to keep the vowel short when the ending begins with a vowel (see Doubling, pp. 79–80 and note that in longer words it is when the short vowel is in a stressed syllable).

sit	sitting
bat	batted
rot	rotten

4. Words ending in *y* or *ie* use *-ied* for the past tense (and *-ies* for the third person present and for plurals), e.g.

try	tried
die	died
hurry	hurries
lady	ladies

Both -y and -ie use *-y* when *-ing* is added — a point not often known by pupils, e.g.

try	trying
die	dying
hurry	hurrying

Apart from this case, words ending in *y* generally change to *i* medially when endings are added, e.g.

	holy day	holiday
	happy	happily, happier, happiest, happiness
	mercy	merciful, merciless
	dry	drily
But	sly	slyly
	shy	shyly

Appendix I

Handwriting

It is important that correct letter production should be established as soon as possible. It is *incorrect* letter production which sometimes results in letters being written facing the wrong way, and sometimes in confusions; in particular, when a child incorrectly starts the letter *d* at the top, he readily confuses it with the letter *b*.

Pupils should be taught the correct place for starting the letter. They can be given samples in the form of cardboard letters which clearly indicate the starting place and the direction to go as illustrated below. The teacher should draw the letter with a light-coloured felt pen.

These can be taken back to the class for practice. In this way a clear basic distinction has been made between *d* and *b*; *d*, unlike most letters with uprights, is not started at the top. If *b* is written ✔ it is, of course, more clearly distinguished from *d*.

A correct starting place also enables the pupil to finish each letter in the best position for starting the next letter, thus laying the foundations for fluent writing.

Alternatively pupils can be taught cursive writing from the beginning, so that they are used to having a hook on each letter. Dyslexic children become extremely confused if there is a complete change to 'double writing' (involving starting the letter in a different place) at a particular stage in school — which is nearly always too early for them. Correct holding of the pen is also important. Flexible plastic pen grips which fit on to a pencil or biro are a reminder of the correct pen-holding position. The pupil should have room on the desk to rest both arms on it, with the left hand holding the book steady, possibly at an angle and to the right of him — whatever he finds comfortable.

Lefthanders in particular should be urged to push the book to the left, with the foot of the page sloping away from them so that they do not adopt a 'hook' position.

When practising letters it is useful for the child to say aloud (verbalise) what he is doing (see Introduction, p. 4).

Alphabet and Dictionary Skills

Work on the alphabet can start quite soon. If it is sung in the following letter groups, the rhymes help to make it memorable:

ÁBĆD ÉFǴ HÍJḰLḾ NÓPQ́ RŚTÚ VẂXÝŹ

Display of the whole alphabet in a 'rainbow' formation or some similar arrangement is a useful way for pupils to become gradually more proficient in its use. It provides a means of learning both the entire sequence and the relative position of groups of letters in a way that can be fun (e.g. remove a letter or rearrange some, and ask the pupil to spot the error; or ask a pupil to find a target letter with his eyes closed). It is better to use lower case letters for this to impress the point that capital letters are to be used only for certain specific purposes.

Pupils can be helped to learn the sequence for dictionary work by dividing it into sections of five or six letters; the English dictionary conveniently divides into four such 'quartiles', viz. A to E, F to M, N to S, T to Z.

Practice can be given with tracking exercises (a variety of such material is available), and with games. By these various devices pupils become confident and are able to answer automatically to questions about sequence.

Dictionary work itself can begin as soon as the pupil reads well enough to use the simplest dictionary available, with the alphabet written out for reference if needed. It can be combined with reading practice and provides a useful focus for oral work. For children who are lacking in verbal skills and general knowledge, it can also be a useful method of extending their vocabulary and showing them that words have 'meanings' which can be defined in different ways.

From the beginning the pupil should be shown how to use the 'quartile' method of searching for words by opening the book at roughly the correct place. This appeals to many children (and adults!), as it reduces the frustration of not being able to find the word quickly.

Early introduction to dictionary work, using dictionaries which have pictures and are 'fun' books (such as the Dr Seuss dictionary), can help a pupil to look on a dictionary as a useful aid. So often the phrase 'Look it up!' is an unwelcome admonition, seen as a sign that some adult is not willing to help.

Books and Materials

This list is not intended to be comprehensive; but the following have been found particularly useful.

Books containing programmes, sentences etc.

Help for Dyslexic Children by T.R. Miles and Elaine Miles. London: Routledge (1983).
Alpha to Omega by Beve Hornsby and Frula Shear. London: Heinemann Educational (1976).†
Spelling Made Easy by Violet Brand, Baldock, Herts.: Egon Press Publishers Ltd, particularly Levels 2 and 3 (1984, 1985).†
Remedial Spelling by Violet Brand. Baldock, Herts.: Egon Press Publishers Ltd (1985).

†These books also have worksheets.

Phonic readers

These have been found valuable when used in conjunction with the *Bangor Dyslexia Teaching System* in the very early stages.
Primary Phonics, and the parallel series *More Primary Phonics* by Barbara Makar. Cambridge, Mass.: Educators Publishing Service.
    Set 1 (10 books in each case) for short vowels.
    Set 2 (10 books in each case) for final *e* and the most common vowel digraphs.
One Way with Words by Anne-Marie Gillam. Bath: Bath Educational Publishers Ltd, 7, Walcot Building, London Road, Bath BA1 6AD.
    (21 books, short vowels, consonant blends, final *e*, 'r' patterns and some basic irregular words).
Tempo books. Harlow, Essex: Longman (recently gone out of print, but still in use).
Fuzzbuzz, Oxford University Press and *Bangers and Mash*, Harlow, Essex: Longman, serve as useful supplementary, partly phonic readers.

Others with a controlled vocabulary are:

High Noon Books, Ann Arbor, PO Box 1, Belford, Northumberland NE70 7JX.
Woodpeckers, Oxford Tree series, Oxford University Press.

Materials and workbooks

Cards for teaching and practising sounds and letters:
Alpha to Omega cards London: Heinemann Educational Books.
Phonic Blends, *Phonic Rummy*. Kenworthy Educational

Boxes and sets of letters:
Edith Norrie Letter Case, Helen Arkell Dyslexia Centre, Frensham, Farnham, Surrey, GU10 3BW.
Word building letters, upper and lower case.
Magnetic plastic letters from branches of Early Learning Centre.
Other plastic letters from Tesco Moulded Plastics, Earl's Barton, Northampton NN6 0JG.

Handwriting books and aids

Pencil grips from Taskmaster, Morris Road, Leicester.
Workbooks and guide cards for teaching and practising letter formation from Ladybird, Taskmaster, LDA and others.

Phonic workbooks

These provide valuable and interesting homework to reinforce and practise what has been taught in the lesson. Those chosen should have the following characteristics:
    Work should be presented in small steps and should require the writing of the whole word not just the filling in of gaps. Presentation should be clear, with plenty of space and good, bold printing, with the spelling point highlighted. There should be plenty of examples at each level, with a chance for the target word to be used in a variety of ways, including reading.

Suggestions:

Sure-Fire Phonics by Ann Williams and Jim Rogerson (books 1–5). Walton-on-Thames: Nelson. Especially useful for younger children and reusable.

Stile Phonics books with self-checking tray and tiles, LDA. Wisbech, Cambs.

Read, Write and Spell by Gillian Nettle and Julia Leech. London: Heinemann Educational Books (four books). Suitable for upper primary school, and (selectively) for lower secondary school.

Exercise Your Spelling by Elizabeth Wood. London: Hodder and Stoughton (three books). Useful at top junior and lower secondary level.

Attack-a-Track by Lynn Lewis. Bath: Bath Educational Publishers.

Tracking exercises by Ann Arbor (address above).

The Book of Letters. An adventure in reading, writing and spelling by Michael Thomson. Wisbech, Cambs: LDA (1989).

There are also worksheets to *Alpha to Omega* and of Violet Brand's *Remedial Spelling*, mentioned above.

Other reading

Understanding Dyslexia by T.R. Miles. Bath: Amethyst Books (1987).

Overcoming Dyslexia by Beve Hornsby. London: Heinemann (1982).

Children's Written Language Difficulties edited by M. Snowling. Windsor: NFER-Nelson (1985).

Children's Reading Problems by Peter Bryant and Lynette Bradley. Oxford, Blackwell (1985).

English Phonetics and Phonology by Peter Roach. Oxford: OUP (1983).

Simple Phonetics for Teachers by Jean Smith and Margaret Bloor. London: Routledge (1985).

Dyslexia — The Pattern of Difficulties by T.R. Miles. Oxford: Blackwell (1983).

Dyslexia a Hundred Years On by T.R. Miles and E. Miles. Milton Keynes: Open University Press (1990).

Our Language by Simeon Potter. Harmondsworth, Middx.: Penguin Books (1950).

Child Language, Learning and Linguistics by David Crystal. London: Edward Arnold (1987).

Specific Learning Difficulties (Dyslexia), A Teacher's Guide by Margaret Crombie. Glasgow: Jordanhill College of Education (1991). (This contains valuable lists of books, materials and software.)

Software

There is a great deal of software for BBC computers which is useful, e.g.

Bangor Hi-Spell, Suites 1,2,3, which complements this teaching programme, Xavier Educational Software, Department of Psychology, UCNW, Bangor, Gwynedd LL57 2DG.

Soap Box, Xavier, as above, for BBC Archimedes.

Fun Phonics, PAVIC Publications, Sheffield Polytechnic.

An Eye for Spelling by Charles Cripps, Living and Learning, Cambridge.

Starspell Plus, Fisher-Marriott.

*These can be adapted to the teacher's own lists of words.

For further information about dyslexia, provision etc., apply to:
The British Dyslexia Association,
98 London Road,
Reading,
Berks RG1 5AU

Part II

The Secondary School Approach: Introduction

The division of the syllabus into two parts does not reflect a clear distinction between 'primary school work' and 'secondary school work'. Any child with a spelling age of less than 7½ years will need to start at the beginning of Part I material, and, alas, there are still some children at this level even in secondary school. Apart from this, even secondary school pupils need to have fully explained to them at the outset the distinction between short vowels and long vowels, so that they are able to handle these key terms, since the distinction is fundamental to English spelling and has far-reaching effects. There may also be points in the earliest work which older pupils have never mastered, for instance -tch and -dge endings; which words have ou and which ow; correct blending of initial consonants (particularly 'l' and 'r' blends); the automatic expectation that c and g will be pronounced with their soft sounds before e, i or y.

However, because of the secondary school pupil's greater familiarity with spelling patterns, the work is likely to be organised differently, with greater emphasis on the pupil knowing all the possible 'choices' of spelling pattern for each sound or at least having a chart of them to which he can refer. At this stage he can absorb longer groups, 'ought' words along with 'ough', or au, aught, ought, and all among the alternative spelling of the 'or' sound.

When presenting early material to the older pupils, the teacher will want from the beginning to include words of more than one syllable — 'ticket', 'kitchen', 'badger', for instance, when they are studying short-vowel words. He will include not just 'time' and 'ride' when teaching i–e, but 'excite', 'decide'. This inevitably involves a study of syllabification at an early stage, as well as a look at simple prefixes and the single long vowel in a prefix such as rē-, prō-, etc.

When starting with the older, more advanced pupil of 13, 14 and upwards, a different outlook seems necessary. It is not possible with such pupils to follow a set programme. That is not to say, of course, that the teacher will not be systematic or structured in his approach, but that he has to determine his priorities and plot his course to suit the need of the individual pupil.

Needless to say it requires an experienced teacher to do this. The basic ideas have to be introduced, but at the same time one has to ensure that the pupil can from the start use polysyllabic words with confidence in his school work so as not to restrict his natural imagination and range of vocabulary. Moreover the plan of work must be related to the pupil's written work for other staff. The dictionary, most probably in a file, will still be retained for the basic structure, but will be slightly different in character, in that different spellings of the same sound, each with a few examples, will have to appear on the same page for reference, but may be put there gradually. There will obviously have to be pages for prefixes and suffixes, and other specific topics. It is better, however, to have subject vocabulary and pupil's own problem words in separate small notebooks, because these are isolated words, not fitted into a structure.

The teacher has to retain some overall framework of the syllabus that he would like to cover so that the lessons do not leave the pupil with some ideas perfected and others entirely neglected. Such a syllabus might comprise:

1. Consolidation of basic work in Part I of the syllabus but with polysyllabic vocabulary (provided in this book).
2. Alternative single-letter and two-letter spellings of consonant sounds (s, ce) etc.; plurals (pp. 50–51).
3. Clear enunciaton of words in speech and recognition of their grammatical function before anything is written down.
4. Doubling (Part I, pp. 12–14, and Part II, pp. 79–80).
5. Function of an e; when to keep an e and when to drop it when adding suffixes (pp. 78–79).
6. Syllabification and stress. Open and closed syllables (p. 50). Word-building and roof–prefix–suffix awareness.
7. Prefixes, simple and more advanced, including the study of their meanings (pp. 62–65).
8. Choice of spelling patterns for vowel sounds (pp. 56–59).
9. Common confusions between similar sounding words and similar sounding endings, e.g.

-ind / -ined
-st / -ssed

10. Suffixes, simple and more advanced (pp. 68–75); various foreign endings, e.g. *-que, -re, -ine* (pp. 70 and 71).
11. Subject vocabulary.
12. Other suffixes easily confused (pp. 69–71).

> *-ery* / *-ary* / *-ory*
> *-ent* / *-ant*
> *-able* / *-ible*

Guidelines for choice should be given wherever possible; in other cases the pupil will list only the most common words.
13. Negative prefixes *in-, il-, im-, ir-, un-* (see p. 62).

It should be noted that there is no set order for teaching this programme, and that the vocabulary will differ with different pupils.

How to start

A good way to begin is to get the pupil to read out aloud work that he has himself written. The teacher can then check the clarity of his enunciation and require him to check if he has indeed written down the sounds that he has spoken, especially not very prominent sounds like the 'grunting' *n* in 'amount'; and whether he has recorded them accurately, i.e. not *t* for *d* or *b* for *p*. When this phonetic correspondence is improved his work becomes much more intelligible to the reader, in particular to his other teachers, and he begins to acquire the habit of *listening*. It can also be checked whether he is applying suffixes which reflect grammatical function, like *-ing* and *-ed*. There are a number of common confusions, e.g. between *their* and *there* and between *where*, *were* and *wear*, which are not just spelling mistakes, but show a lack of appreciation of grammatical distinctions. Finally the pupil has to check whether he is recording the correct number of syllables in words, which leads to a study of syllabification. All this is a question of pronouncing correctly and listening critically.

Current written work must not, of course, be allowed to dictate the course of the lesson; the pupil must be able to see that he is learning general principles and that there is a sense of direction and purpose. Correcting past mistakes is apt to be of little interest unless it offers hope of knowing how to proceed in the future.

The teacher will have to consider next the fact that there are various alternative ways of spelling the same sound, both for consonants and for vowels, which leads him to, e.g.

— The choice of alternative spellings of certain simple consonant sounds.
  soft *s* / soft *c*
  k / *c* / *ck*
  j / soft *g*
  hard *s* / *z*
  y / *i*   Changes of *y* to *i* (see Part I).

— Choices of vowel spellings for the same sound — the pupil has to learn to think in terms of probabilities.

General principles which must be given priority, because of their wide relevance, are

— When to drop or not to drop an *e* when adding a suffix (see 'Dropping an <u>e</u>', pp. 78–79)
— Roots, prefixes and suffixes must be introduced in order to engage in most valuable exercises in word-building. The technique is to start either with a short word and change it to related longer words, or to start with a root and add different prefixes and suffixes, e.g.
  Short words:
  Start with 'image' — turn it into 'imagination'
                     — turn it into 'imaginary'
                     — turn it into 'imagine'

Lessons that can be learnt from this are:
The unclear *a* in 'image' becomes clearly heard in a related word.
This *a* determines that the suffix is *-ary* rather than *-ery*.
  -ine is an ending found in words of French origin without long *i* pronunciation (see p. 71).

Start with 'sign' — turn it into 'signal'
                  — turn it into 'resignation', 'resign', 'designation', 'design', 'assignation', 'assign', 'assignment'
                  — turn it into 'signature'

Lessons to be learnt from this are:

The sometimes silent *g* is clearly heard in other related words.

The *a* in the 'ation' nouns is a clue to the unclear *a* in 'signature'.

Roots:

Start with '-struct-' — add different prefixes *con-, de-, in-, ob- sub-, super-*

— add different suffixes *-ure, -ion, -ing, -or, -ive*

Lessons to be learnt are:

To look for common roots in words and understand their meanings.

To identify prefixes and suffixes and understand their meanings.

It is much more profitable to study related words in this way and derive general principles than to correct individual words. The teacher can start the exercise from a single word in a piece of written work which has caused problems and branch out from there.

Resource material in this book

A word of explanation is needed about the material in the rest of this book. The extensive lists of words to be found, particularly in Sections 7 and 8, and in the suffix section, Section 10, are not there to be taught in their entirety. From them the teacher can select, say, half a dozen words of a pattern that she or he thinks most suitable for the pupil whom she or he is teaching. It is not easy to think them up on the spur of the moment. Or when a certain word comes up as a problem in written work, she or he can avoid teaching that word in isolation by consulting the pattern that it belongs to. For instance, if the problem word is 'hoarse' it is much better to teach 'coarse' too, and maybe even 'hoard' and 'board' (and 'cupboard'). There are after all few words of that pattern with a letter after the *oar*. If some are already known, so much the better. Similarly if reminding the pupil of the *e* on the end of 'examine', why not point out that a couple of other verbs of French origin end in the same way, viz. 'imagine', 'determine'?

From time to time, also the teacher will find explanations which will help the pupil, e.g. the *-ery* ending denotes 'stock-in-trade' as in 'grocery', 'stationery' (thus distinguishing it from 'stationary').

There is detailed guidance on the teaching of prefixes and suffixes.

Reading

The emphasis is necessarily different at the secondary school stage. With the young child one has to build a sound foundation of connexion between the spoken words and the written letters so that he clearly sees one as *corresponding to* the other.

By secondary school, foundations should have been laid and the first year pupil will be reading at least at a 9 year level or indeed higher if he is of above average ability. Whatever his standard of reading he has to read and appreciate materials of quite a high level and to do this he must be interested and have the confidence to tackle even difficult material with the expectation of extracting the meaning.

The teacher should supply judicious help and teach a range of techniques which the pupil can apply to help himself and thus ensure a high degree of accuracy.

(a) *Direct help*

Supplying difficult words.

Reading alternately with the pupil.

Reading the first chapter, page or paragraph to introduce the story and the book's background and characters.

(b) *Techniques*

Division of long words with finger by blocking off parts.

Identification of prefixes and suffixes.

Recognition of vowel sound produced by vowel digraphs.

Systematic practice in word attack skills by reading specially prepared lists of words. (This may well link with the spelling points being taught.)

Careful examination of beginning of long words, and of short words.

Use of clues such as capital letters, chapter headings,
   titles and pictures.
Reading from one full stop to the next so that the task is
   manageable (this also helps fluency).
Reading on past a word that perplexes to get
   contextual help for its identification.

(c) *Training in accurate reading habits*
Oral questions on passages which are prepared by the
   pupil for teacher to answer. (Teacher has 1–2
   minutes to skim!!)
Oral questions from teacher.
Practice in fast reading of words, e.g. with Phonic
   Rummy Cards. (Can be turned into a game that the
   pupil always wins.)
Practice with nonsense words so as to ensure that letter
   sounds, vowel digraphs, etc., are well known.
Insistence on careful observation of punctuation,
   especially where it affects meaning.
Practice at reading verse with a strong rhythm, limericks,
   modern verse.
Manipulation of words for fun — crosswords, etc.

More general aspects of written work

The pupil of 13, 14 upwards not only needs special help
with reading and spelling, but also:

1. Oral and listening skills for the GCSE oral English
   assessment and future career interviews.
2. Guidance in time management, organising and
   presenting work, particularly GCSE coursework.
3. Help with coherent expression and accurate
   answers when answering comprehension papers.
4. Practice in summarising passages.
5. Guidance on essay writing: identifying different types
   of writing; planning etc.
6. Help with letter-writing and form-filling.
7. Tuitiion and practice in one-word note-taking.
8. Techniques in handling of examination papers.

One-word note-taking

This technique can be practised with a tape-recorder.
The procedure is as follows:

1. Listen to the tape carefully and write down key
   words.
2. At the end read through the words and add any
   extra information remembered.
3. Turn each word into a phrase.
4. Write up the phrases into a paragraph.

In due course the pupil will progress to writing down
phrases in the first place. This is a highly skilled
technique leading to good note-taking, since the close
attention and constructive thought required will give a
much better basis for revision than the automatic
recording of undigested material.

Study skills book list

Strategies for Studying by M. Coles and C. White.
   London: Collins Educational (1985).
English for G.S.C.E. by J.B. Griffin and T.M. Sullivan.
   London: Unwin and Hyman (1985).
Starting to Teach Study Skills by Douglas Hamblin.
   Oxford: Basil Backwell (1986).
Use Your Head by Tony Buzan. London: Ariel Books,
   distributed BBC (1982).
Pergamon Dictionary of Perfect Spelling. Leeds: Arnold-
   Wheaton (1977; reprint 1987).
Mastering Study Skills by R. Freeman. Basingstoke:
   Macmillan Educational (1990).
'Memory and Spelling' — a resource sheet — in
   Unscrambling Spelling by Cynthia Klein.
   Sevenoaks, Kent: Hodder and Stoughton (1990).
Your Memory: A user's guide by Alan Baddeley.
   Harmondsworth: Penguin (1982).
'Study skills teaching at secondary school' by Dorothy
   Gilroy. In *Dyslexia Contact* 10, No. 2 (Dec. 1991).

Section 7

Basic Word Structure, Short Vowels and Final *e*

Syllabification and stress

Clear articulation and counting of the successive 'bits' of a word helps pupils not to omit parts of a word in writing. The syllables can be tapped out before the word is commenced. It is also useful practice to divide up words either with dividing lines or physically, with scissors, when they can also be reassembled. It is, however, possible to put the dividing lines at slightly different points according to the principle of division:

1. To reflect the way in which we naturally say the word. This would probably involve dividing the word 'extra' *e-xtra*, but such a division does not particularly help spelling because the consonant combination is then even more difficult to sort out, and identification of the prefix is obscured.

2. To assist the identification of long and short vowels, diphthongs, 'r' combinations etc. It is convenient to classify syllables into six categories:

(a)　Closed syllables — where there is a consonant at the end of the syllable and the vowel is usually short, e.g. 'con/tent'.
(b)　Open syllables — where there is a vowel at the end of a syllable, and the vowel is usually long, e.g. 'pi/lot'.
(c)　Vowel–consonant–e — where the vowel is usually long, e.g. 'state/ment'.
(d)　Diphthong — where the vowel is usually long, e.g. 'plea/sing'.
(e)　-le syllable — e.g. 'ta/ble'.
(f)　'r' combination — where the *r* affects the vowel pronunciation;
　　　'w' combination — where the *w* affects the vowel pronunciation;
　　　'y' combination — where the *y* affects the vowel pronunciation;
　　　e.g. 'for/tune', 'aw/ful', 'pay/ment'.

This particularly assists reading since it makes the consonant combinations more manageable and helps decisions on vowel pronunciation. It does not fit well with words of foreign origin which do not follow a doubling principle (particularly words derived from Greek); such words often contain just one consonant after a single vowel pronounced short e.g. 'comic', 'camel'. (See lists in 'Doubling' section, p. 80.) It may also conflict with recognition of suffixes, e.g. 'stan/ding'.

3. It is helpful, particularly at the secondary stage, to divide words into prefix–root–suffix, perhaps in order to compare the same root in different words, thus dividing the word into *morphemes*, e.g.

se- *par*-ate	a- *spir*-ate
dis- *par*-ate	in- *spir*-ation
pre- *par*-ation	con- *spir*-acy

where division according to principles in (2) above would be less helpful.

It is important sometimes, also, for the pupil to consider where the stress falls on a word. The doubling of consonants after a short vowel is a practice that applies to syllables which are stressed. Stress or lack of it changes the pronunciation of vowels in prefixes and makes them difficult to identify; suffixes lose clarity of pronunciation and vowel sounds and consonant sounds are corrupted by lack of stress, common in the last syllable of a word.

Dyslexics often find this matter of stress difficult, as they do not consciously reflect on speech characteristics.

Plurals

1. Words ending in *-ss*, *-zz*, *-sh*, *-ch*, *-x* have plurals in *-es*, since it is impossible to pronounce an *s* immediately after these endings; e.g.

crosses　　buzzes　　brushes　　benches　　foxes

2. Some words ending in -o have plurals in -es. Since -o is not an English ending the addition of an s looks strange and invites a short-vowel pronunciation; however, as more words ending with -o have come into the language, it has become acceptable, and there is a dwindling number of words which demand an e. Here are some common ones:

tomatoes	echoes	cargoes	volcanoes
potatoes	heroes	embargoes	vetoes
			Negroes

If the dictionary does not give an -oes plural, one can assume that -os is permissible.

3. Many words ending in -f have -ves plurals, which are easier to pronounce, and the difference should be heard in the oral language. In some cases both alternatives are found.

elf	elves	scarf	scarves (or scarfs)
self	selves	wharf	wharves (or wharfs)
shelf	shelves	hoof	hooves (or hoofs)
half	halves	loaf	loaves
calf	calves	leaf	leaves
wolf	wolves	sheaf	sheaves

dwarf	dwarfs	gulf	gulfs
roof	roofs		
proof	proofs		
turf	turfs		
waif	waifs		
oaf	oafs		
chief	chiefs		
grief	griefs		
brief	briefs		
belief	beliefs		

Some of these last have related verbs which use a -ve ending.

4. Words ending in -y have plurals in -ies, except those ending in the combinations -ay, -ey, -oy, -uy, which add s only, e.g.

spy	spies	day	days	key	keys
pony	ponies	boy	boys	guy	guys

5. A few words stay the same in singular and plural, e.g.

sheep	deer	grouse	salmon	fish

6. Words with irregular plurals:

child	children	mouse	mice
man	men	goose	geese
woman	women	ox	oxen
foot	feet		

Short-vowel patterns with simple prefixes and suffixes

Pupils should be able to write these from dictation if they listen carefully.

On the next page words have been put in groups containing words with the same *root*, which is the main short-vowel syllable. A limited number of prefixes have been employed such as might easily be introduced at an early stage, since they can be written down from the sound. Suffixes have been carefully controlled; thus words of similar pattern ending in -et are included (but none ending in, for example, -ot or -at since that might cause confusion in view of the colourless sound of the vowel (schwa)). The final syllable must be pronounced naturally in dictation.

No words have been included which need a double consonant, since it is assumed that that principle will be taught a little later. Consequently the opportunity has been taken to demonstrate that a *single* consonant after a short vowel is particularly common in words ending in -ic, -id, -ish (see 'Doubling' section, p. 80).

Other short-vowel words

chestnut	dumpling	dolphin	culprit
problem	pumpkin	mistress	arithmetic
petrol	husband	compliment	method
pistol	himself	establishment	
goblin	children	astonishment	
kidnap	hundred	ransack	

a	e		i		o	wa/qua	u	wo
began	upset	distress	begin	cricket	respond	was	begun	won
banish	regret	member	admit	chicken	abolish	wander	dusty	wonder
vanish	shelter	September	submit	kitchen	rocky	wash	rusty	
blanket	enter	November	refit	fidget	frosty	wasp	crusty	
expand	plenty	selfish	limit	wicked	monster	swan	trusty	
handy	envy	perish	exit		oxen	swallow	disgust	
sandy	twenty	helpful	prefix		longest	want	ugly	
gander	empty	velvet	finish		hovel	what	clumsy	
pansy	depend	recent	diminish		topic	watch	under	
panic	defend		minister		tonic	wad	thunder	
banquet	intend		windy		ironic	waltz	understand	
frantic	extend		winter		exotic	swap	hunter	
transatlantic	invent		linger		pocket	squad	hunger	
relax	prevent		finger		socket	squash	number	
exact	absent		clinic		rocket	squabble	bumpy	
contract	resent		critic		lobster	quality	jumpy	
extract	consent		timid		lodger	quantity	grumpy	
subtract	present (verb)		liquid		solid	quarry	dumpy	
inhabit	content		vivid				trumpet	
establish	discontent		rigid				public	
radish	extent		sister				publish	
gravel	index		misty				result	
travel	expect		exist				insult	
fragment	respect		insist				conduct	
sapling	inspect		consist				construct	
chapter	suspect		milky				instruct	
gather	prospect		silky				abrupt	
jacket	direct		risky				discuss	
packet	erect		fifty				budget	
bracket	insect		sixty					
satchel	elect		victim				input	
badger	detect		impish					
gadget	object		uphill					
acid	subject		deliver					
	project		sliver					
	request		convict					
	inquest		conflict					
	conquest		extinct					
	detest		distinct					
	except		illness					
	confess		dismiss					
	express		ticket					
	progress		wicket					

Reminder of short-vowel endings

back/bake
itch/each
edge/age

Other ways of spelling short vowels

ea / ɛ /		o = / ʌ /*	
head	breast	son	compass
dead	peasant	ton	borough
read (past)	pleasant	tongue	thorough
lead (metal)	measure	London	come
ready	treasure	Monday	some
already	jealous	front	done
steady	realm	among	none
instead	breadth	dozen	one
bread		other	once
thread		another	
tread		brother	
dread		mother	
spread		smother	
meadow		nothing	
feather		monk	
heather		cover	
leather		plover	
weather		oven	
death		govern	
breath		shovel	
heavy		slovenly	
heaven		above	
deaf		love	
health		glove	
stealth		dove	
threat		mongrel	
sweater		monkey	
meant		honey	
breakfast		money	
weapon		stomach	
		colour	
		comfort	

/ ʊ / (short oo)	
good etc.	bullet
look etc.	pullet
foot	bullock
wool	pudding
bull	cushion
full	sugar
pull	wolf
bush	woman
push	bosom
put	could
butcher	would
	should

/ ɛ /	/ ɪ /	/ ɒ /	/ ʌ /
any	niche	sausage	touch
many	sieve	fault	young
says	build	laurel	rough
said	England	yacht	tough
Thames	English	knowledge	enough
leisure	breeches	cough	country
heifer	women	trough	cousin
leopard	busy		courage
friend			couple
			double
			trouble
			nourish
			does
			blood
			flood

Note: 'niche' is sometimes pronounced /niʃ/.

y words

myth	system	lyric	style
hymn	symbol	cynic	tyre
lynch	symptom	cymbal	type
crystal	syrup	cyclamen	pyre
cylinder	sympathy	pyramid	scythe
physics	syllable	nymph	cycle
catalyst	symphony	rhythm	pylon
analyst	syringe	mystery	python
	sycamore	Olympic	cyclone
			hydrant
			typhoon

*For *wo* words see Part I, pp. 14–15 and Part II, pp. 52, 58.

Final *e* pattern words with simple prefixes and suffixes

a–e	*e–e*	*i–e*	*o–e*	*u–e*
debate	complete	invite	promote	dispute
relate	concrete	unite	devote	execute
translate	obsolete	ignite	explode	minute (small)
statement	athlete	excite	provoke	astute
grateful	theme	recite	token	dilute
became	extreme	decide	broken	costume
shameful	supreme	provide	awoke	volume
invade	impede	divide	alone	resume
grenade	centipede	beside	telephone	assume
comrade	recede	inside	hopeful	include
mistake	stampede	dislike	open	exclude
waken	trapeze	revive	impose	conclude
shaken	scene	alive	expose	protrude
behave	scheme	prescribe	compose	rebuke
pavement	intervene	combine	disclose	tubeless
insane	serene	confine	enclose	excuse
replace	here	divine	closely	refuse
disgrace	sphere	decline	clothes	confuse
embrace	adhere	ninety		abuse
engage	interfere	advise	deplore*	amuse
declare		despise	implore	accuse
prepare		advice	explore	reduce
beware		oblige	restore	produce
compare		respite	ignore	deduce
		ignite	sycamore	refuge
		finite		deluge
		admire		Tuesday
		desire		pure
		empire		endure
		retire		procure
		inquire		secure
		require		insure
		entire		

*Note that -*ore* has the same sound as *or* (see p. 15), and *not* the long 'o' sound.

Section 8

The Other Basic Vowel Patterns, *r* Combinations and Consonant Groups

Long-vowel-sound spelling choices

Secondary school pupils are already acquainted with a large variety of vowel digraphs and get thoroughly confused between them. It takes time to sort out all this confusion, and in the meanwhile a reference chart with key words for each spelling possibility can be given to them to remind them of the alternatives.

Key words should be chosen to suit the pupil's interest if possible. For instance 'referee', 'team', 'field' might be memorable to a sports enthusiast. Words might also be chosen in order to pinpoint one of a pair of homophones, e.g. 'pain' for *ai*. The lists given here, therefore, should be regarded only as samples to indicate the alternatives available.

There are numerous ways of spelling long a, e, i, o, u sounds, so it is convenient to list these first.

a sound	*e sound*	*i sound*	*o sound*	*u/oo sound*
/ eɪ /	/ iː /	/ aɪ /	/ əʊ /	/ uː / or /juː/
name*	these	pipe*	home*	tube*
say	see	pie	toe	rule*
train	green	my	boat	cue
they	sea	high	snow	glue
vein	team	dye	most	few
great	field	style	po-tato	Jew
paper	ceiling	kind		moon
	re-cent	pi-lot		soup
		py-lon		fruit
				tunic

*See p. 54 for such words. Lists of words with /uː/ sound will be found on the next page.

Other spellings of these sounds which are less frequent

straight	key	eye	do, to, two, who
eight	quay	buy	you
weight	people	guy	shoe, canoe
freight	seize	height	view
reign	sheik	aisle	beauty
neigh	paeony†	climb	move, prove
neighbour	archaeology†	either	lose, whose
gaol	amoeba†	neither	tomb, womb
gauge			truth
suede		sew	feud, neutral,
aye (ever)		yolk	queue
precis		folk	rheumatic
		brooch	pneumatic
		mauve	
		only	
		bureau	
		chauffeur	

'Either' and 'neither' are pronounced with a long 'e' sound by some.

'Shoulder' and 'soul' have an 'o' sound modified by the *l*, like 'roll'.

Vowel digraphs for other vowel sounds

oy/oi		*ow/ou*	
boy	boil	cow	out
royal	toilet	fowl	south
oyster	noise	brown	cloud
voyage	poignant	flower	ground
buoy			flour
destroy			mouth
employ			plough
enjoy			house
ploy			mountain
deploy			crouch
annoy			
alloy			

For aw/au lists see p. 58.

† *ae* and *oe* are regular spellings of diphthongs found in technical terms derived from Latin and Greek.

Words having spelling patterns other than oo or u–e for u sounds

ue	ew	ou / uː /	ui
rue	dew	youth	suit
sue	few	soup	fruit
due	hew	group	cruise
cue	new	coup	bruise
blue	blew	through	juice
clue	threw	ghoul	sluice
glue	knew	route	nuisance
true	slew	routine	recruit
Tuesday	drew		
value	flew		*eu*
venue	stew		feud
argue	chew		neutral
residue	crew		neutron
virtue	screw		queue
issue	yew		
tissue	view		
subdue	phew		
statue	mews		
pursue	newt		
avenue	pewter		
continue	nephew		
rescue	mildew		
	curfew		
	Andrew		

'r' combinations

The combination of a single vowel with *r* causes a modification of that vowel similar to that found with *l*.

A single vowel before *double r* preceding a suffix beginning with a vowel usually reverts to the short vowel sound.

A single vowel before *single r* preceding a suffix beginning with a vowel has a long sound; a word ending with *-ore* drops the e.

This follows the usual doubling principle, e.g.

marry	berry	mirror	sorry	hurry
vary	query	wiry	story	fury

scoring, storage

In a few words the *double r* preserves the original vowel sound of the base word, which emphasises the link with it, e.g.

starry (like a star), furry (like fur)

er sounds

er	ir	ur	
-er ending	sir	fur	burden
her	stir	blur	surname
term	fir	purr	surprise
germ	birch	burn	surface
kerb	girl	turn	surgeon
herb	bird	spur	surround
jerk	first	cur	murder
stern	third	hurl	murmur
serve	thirteen	purse	turnip
nerve	thirty	curse	nurse(ry)
swerve	birth	church	turkey
verse	birthday	hurt	turtle
herd	mirth	spurt	disturb
(shepherd)	shirt	turf	absurd
person	skirt	surf	burglar
certain	squirt	burst	sturdy
jersey	circle	urge	surplus
alert	circus	urgent	curtain
serpent	dirt	purple	Thursday
merchant	dirty	purpose	Saturday
servant	thirsty	pursue	urban
service	firm	furnish	turban
refer	confirm	furnace	purchase
infer	whirl	further	
prefer	whirlpool		*ear*
defer	virtue	*wor*	earth
mercy		word	learn
superb	*our*	work	earnest
	journey	worm	search
were	journal	world	research
	courtesy	worse	heard
	courteous	worst	early
		worth	pearl
		worship	Earl

(The teaching of 'shepherd' follows naturally from 'herd', even though the pronunciation is not fully 'er'.)

or sounds

war/quar	au	oar	aw
war	Paul	oar	saw
warm	haul	roar	jaw
warn	cause	soar	law
award	pause	board	paw
reward	haunt	cupboard	drawer
wardrobe	jaunt	hoard	straw
warden	gaunt	coarse	claw
swarm	launch	hoarse	(g)naw
dwarf	staunch		shawl
towards	sauce	*our*	crawl
(backwards)	saucer	four	scrawl
(forwards)	taut	court	sprawl
(afterwards)	laundry	course	bawl (shout)
wart	assault	pour	brawl
quart	fraud	source	dawn
quartz	applaud	resources	fawn
wharf	ex(h)aust		lawn
	auction	your	pawn
or	caution		drawn
or	autumn	*augh*	prawn
for	August	caught	spawn
nor	authority	taught	awful
fortune	audio	naughty	awe
important etc.	audible	haughty	hawk
	audit	daughter	squawk
ore	audition	slaughter	awkward
more		distraught	dawdle
core			
bore		broad	
sore (hurt)	*all*	abroad	
tore	all		
wore	ball	*alk*	*ough*
fore	call	talk	bought
score	fall	walk	brought
shore	pall	chalk	thought
before	tall	stalk (flower)	ought
ignore	small		fought
implore	wall	*ald*	nought
restore	stall	bald	sought
adore	squall	scald	wrought iron
	walnut		
	walrus	*water*	door
			floor

Note that in some parts of the country 'poor', 'moor', 'boor' are also pronounced like 'door', 'floor'. Whether 'your' is included also depends on individual pronunciation.

The teaching of 'backward', 'forward', 'afterwards' follows naturally from 'towards' even though pronounced with a schwa.

alt words are usually pronounced with / ɒ / sound, e.g. 'salt', 'halt', 'malt', 'alter', 'falter', 'halter'.

/ɛə/ sounds

are	air	ear
bare	air	bear
care	fair (light)	pear
dare	fair (big dipper)	tear
fare (bus)	fair (just)	wear
fare (food)	fair (no rain)	swear
welfare	fairy	
hare (animal)	hair (head)	
mare (animal)	pair (two)	
share	stairs	
stare (look)	chair	
scare	flair	
spare	repair	
square	despair	
aware	prairie	there
compare	affair	where
prepare	flair	
parents	repair	their
beware	lair	heir
area	cairn	

vary
wary

Note: layer, player, prayer, mayor.

ear sounds

eer	*ear*	*ere*	*ier*
deer	ear	here	pier
beer	hear	mere	tier
jeer	dear	sphere	fierce
peer	fear	adhere	pierce
veer	gear	austere	
steer	near	interfere	
queer	rear	sincere(ly)	
sheer (steep)	year		
	clear		
	spear		
	shears		
	appear		
	arrears		

Note: some people pronounce year like 'earth'.

Silent letters

(For initial silent letters *gn, kn, wr* see Part I, p. 32).

b	*h*	*g*	*t*
debt	heir	sign	often
doubt	honest	resign	soften
subtle	honour	design	Christmas
	hour	assignment	christen
	exhaust	consignment	fasten
	exhibit	reign	hasten
		foreign	listen
			glisten

mb	*mn*	*p*	moisten
bomb	damn	receipt	castle
dumb	condemn		nestle
thumb	hymn		trestle
crumb	column	*w*	(w)restle
numb	solemn	answer	bristle
plumber	Autumn	who	gristle
succumb		whom	whistle
aplomb	*ps*	whose	thistle
limb	psalm	whole	jostle
comb	psychology	sword	hustle
tomb	psychiatry		bustle
womb	psychic		rustle
	pseudonym		mortgage

Other two-letter, one-sound combinations

ph		*ch = /k/ (Greek ch)*	
elephant	prophet	chasm	Christian
alphabet	triumph	chaos	Christmas
telephone	sphere	orchestra	echo
graph	phial	orchid	chorus
paragraph	pheasant	stomach	chord
telegraph	physics	architect	choir
photograph	phantom	character	chemist
Geography	semaphore	chrome	chiropodist
nephew	phrase	scheme	school
hyphen	phase	technical	chronic
philosophy	emphasis	mechanical	chronicle
		chrysanthemum	

qu = /k/	*ch = / ʃ / (French ch)*	
quay	machine	chic
queue	chute	chamois
quiche	cache	champagne
quoit	chassis	charade
	chauffeur	chef
(-que ending p. 65)	chalet	charlatan
	creche	

Note: for list of words in which *sc = /s/* before *e, i, y*, see Part I, p. 32.

Section 9

Prefixes

Identification of prefixes is a valuable aid towards reading long unfamiliar words. It is also important for spelling, since listening for the vowel sound in a prefix is not an infallible guide; for a number of reasons variations occur in the pronunciation of the same prefix in different words (compare 'pronoun' and 'profit', 'refer' and 'reference'). In some cases, when the prefix is in an unstressed syllable, different prefixes may be indistinguishable by sound alone. Identification of the prefix on other grounds is therefore necessary to decide both on the vowel to write and whether double consonants have to be written.

1. Single-syllable prefixes ending in a vowel

The same prefix may be found pronounced with a long or short vowel or with a schwa in different words (see examples below). Double consonants are never used, even after a short vowel. There may, however, be alternative forms ending in a consonant, and for the behaviour of these see next column.

	pre	– before	e.g. prefect, preference, prevent
	re	– back	rebate, relegate, report
	de	– down (from)	defect, demonstrate, decide
(dis)	di	– in different directions	dilate, diligent, divide
	pro	– on behalf of	programme, profit, provide
(ex)	e	– out (of)	evoke, eminent, elect
(ab)	a	– away from	alien, avert

These are all Latin prefixes. The last of these is confusable with ad = to (for which see 2(d), next column), and also with the following:

a	– without (Greek)	e.g. apathy
a	– on (Anglo–Saxon)	ablaze
a	– to (French, from Latin ad)	avenue

The third of these is not very common. All of them, however, have short vowels.

Note: The words 'acute' and 'divine' do not in fact begin with a prefix; ac and div are roots.

2. Single-syllable prefixes ending with a consonant

These often assimilate final consonants to the first letter of the root. Prefixes ending with the same sound (whatever their language of origin) tend to make the same phonetic changes.

(a) Ending in /n/ — in, en, con, syn
n changes to m before b, p, m; assimilates to b, r, e.g.

engage, embrace, emperor
inactive, imbibe, important, immense, illusion, irrigate
convince, combine, company, commotion, collect, correct
syntax, symbol, sympathy, symmetry, syllable

Note: The word 'enough' does not in fact have a prefix; the root has lost its initial g. (Old English was 'genog'.)

(b) Ending in /s/ — dis, ex
s, x, assimilate to f, e.g.
dislike, difficult
expel, effect

(c) Ending in /b/ — sub, ob
b assimilates to c, g, f, p; is lost before two consonants, e.g.
submit, succour, suggest, suffer, support, suspect, sustain
object, occur, offer, oppose

Note: The prefix sur (French from Latin super), when followed by a root beginning with r can be mistaken for an assimilation of sub, e.g. as in 'surrender' and 'surround'. In fact b does not assimilate to r.

(d) Ending in /d/ — ad
d assimilates frequently to b, c, f, g, l, n, r, s, t; is lost before two or more consonants; becomes c before q; e.g.
advance, abbreviate, accept, affect, aggression, allow, announce, arrest, assist, attend, ascend, acquire

Confusable prefixes

The two Latin prefixes ab (a) and ad and the three

different *a* prefixes, Greek, Anglo–Saxon and French, have already been mentioned.

Two other Latin prefixes which are easily confused are *de* and *di* (*dis*), because when the stress is not on the prefix, the vowels lose their value and both come out as / də /. If there is an *s*, the question is whether it belongs to the prefix or the root. The *s* may appear in an assimilated form, as *diff* (see (b) above). Compare:

'dis-turb' and 'de-scend'
'dif-ferent' and 'de-fend'

This can often be determined by comparing other words with the same root, e.g.

de-cide	cf. 'in-cident'
de-scend	cf. 'a-scend'
de-sign	cf. 're-sign'
de-spair	cf. 'a-spiration'
de-stroy	cf. 'con-struct'

There is the occasional word where the *s* of *dis* has been lost, and these words have to be especially noted, e.g. 'diminish' and 'divide'. (There is no current English word beginning *disv*, which is rather hard to pronounce.)

The meaning of the two prefixes should also be noted to assist in their identification:

de	=	down, down from
dis, di	=	apart

There are also pairs of prefixes which are rather similar and might never have been clearly differentiated in oral language by the pupil:

Latin *ante* — before	Latin *inter* — between
Greek *anti* — against	Latin *intro* — inward

Latin *con* — with, among, together	Greek *hypo* — below
Latin *contra* — against	Greek *hyper* — above

Anglo-Saxon *fore*	— previous
Anglo-Saxon *for*	— used to intensify, e.g. 'forswear'
	— used to negate, e.g. 'forget'

Anglo-Saxon, Latin and Greek prefixes

1. Anglo–Saxon prefixes in use in English

Prefix	Meaning	Example
a-	on	ablaze
be-	1. intransitive > transitive	bemoan
(derived	2. intensifying meaning	bedaub
from 'by')	3. modification of transitive	behold
by- bye-	away from main purpose	bystander, byelaw
down-		downstream
for-	1. intensive	forgive
	2. privative	forget
fore-	previous	foretaste
mis-	wrongly	mistake
over-		overcome
un-	1. reversal or deprivation related to Latin *in-*, Greek *an-*	unearth
	2. Intensifying meaning expressed in root	unloose
	3. Strong negative > positive	unkind
under-		underestimate
up-		upstart
with-	over, against	withstand, e.g. 'fight with'

Note: 'forego' is due to confusion with *fore-*, and should logically be 'forgo'.

2. Latin and Greek prefixes in use in English

There are many cases of parallel prefixes from Latin and Greek with similar meanings *both* in use in English. In these cases the Greek one is more likely to be used for exact technical, scientific, medical and mathematical terms — since after all many of these disciplines originated with the Greeks, and in the Renaissance scholars turned to that language when coining new terms.

Those prefixes where a final consonant is likely to assimilate with the first letter of the root, often producing a double consonant, have been marked with an asterisk.

Latin prefix	Example	Greek prefix	Example	Meaning of prefix
a-, ab-, abs-	abrupt	*apo-*	apology	away from
*ad	admit			to
ambi-	ambiguous	*amphi*	amphitheatre	on both sides
ante-	antedate			before
circum-	circumstance	*peri-*	perimeter	round
*con-	congress	**syn-*	syntax	with, among, together
contra-	contradict	*anti-, ant-*	antidote	against
counter-	counteract			
de-	descend	*cata-*	catalyst	down (from)
dis-	disperse			in different directions
ex-, e-	exit	*ek-, ex-*	exodus	out
extra	extravagant	*exo-*	exogamy	outside
*in-	inept	*an-, a-*	anomaly, apathy	negative
*in- (or *en-* French)	induce	**en-*	energy	in
inter-	interfere			between
intro-	introduce	*endo-*	endocrine	within
non-	nonconductor			not
*ob-	object			up against
pen-	penultimate			almost
per-	percolator	*dia-*	diameter	through
post-	postscript	*meta-*	metabolism	after
				(Greek 'meta' contains idea of change as well)
pre-	precede	*pro-*	programme	before
re-	return	*ana-*	anagram	back
retro-	retrograde			
*sub-	submarine	*hypo-*	hypodermic	under
super-	supervise	*hyper-*	hyperactive	above
(or *sur-* French)	surround			
trans-	transfer	*dia-*	diagonal	across
ultra-	ultraviolet			beyond
		para-	parallel	alongside
		dys-	dyslexia	with difficulty

Numerical Latin and Greek prefixes

Latin prefix	Example	Greek prefix	Example	Meaning of prefix
uni-	uniform	*mono-*	monologue	one
bi-, bis-	biped	*dy-*	(no common word)	two
	biscuit			
tri-	trident	*tri-*	tricycle	three
quadr-	quadrangle	*tetr(a)-*	tetragon	four
quin(t)-	quintet	*pent-*	pentagon	five
sex(t)-	sextant	*hex-*	hexameter	six
sept-	September	*hept-*	heptagon	seven
octo-	October	*octa-*	octagon	eight
nov-	November	*ennea-*	(no common word)	nine
decem-	December	*deca-*	decathlon	ten
centi-	centipede	*hecto-* (hecato)	hectogramme	a hundred
mille-	millennium	*chili-*	(no common word)	a thousand
multi-	multigrade	*poly-*	polytechnic	many
semi-	semicircle	*hemi-*	hemisphere	half

Originally September, October, November and
December were the seventh, eighth, ninth and tenth
months of the year, until 'July' and 'August' — named
after Julius Caesar and Augustus Caesar — were
inserted, which brought the total up to twelve.

Section 10

Suffixes and Other Endings

English words have strong stresses in early syllables, and this has the effect of discouraging clear articulation in later, and especially in final, syllables. This becomes a major cause of spelling problems, as follows:

1. Vowels in a final syllable lose their individual character, and are pronounced with a schwa sound / ə /, making a wide range of endings indistinguishable by sound. Here are some examples:

> tartan, curtain, kitten, pattern, foreign, satin, button, stubborn, Whitsun.
> normal, novel, pencil, petrol, consul, noble
> atlas, compass, carcase, prowess, thesis, notice, treatise, thermos, famous, crocus, lettuce
> carat, carpet, credit, carrot, halibut, moderate, definite, minute

Groups of words posing these problems will be considered in the first part of this section, pp. 68–71. Obviously some are more common than others, and some have definite links which help; for instance -al and -ous are adjective endings.

2. Dental sounds (t, d) and sibilants at the end of a root tend to combine with link vowels to form fricatives and affricatives (/ʃ/, /ʒ/ , /tʃ/ ,/dʒ/), which are spelled in different ways in accordance with their origins, e.g.

> mention, version, suspicion, soldier, picture, measure, gradual
> noxious, anxious

Groups of words posing these problems are dealt with in the second part of this section, pp. 66–8. Since -ti combinations are the most common, these have to be stressed most. Guidelines can be given in some other cases, e.g. by reference to other words from the same root in which the consonants have not suffered in this way.

3. Link vowels between the root and the suffix lose their individual character, and are indistinguishable in sound, e.g.

immed *i* ate, court *e* ous

For words with these problems see pp. 74–75.

1. Vowel identification problems in the suffix

Words have not been included if the vowel is clearly pronounced because there is some stress on the last syllable, e.g. 'success', 'expose'.

-ace	-ice	-erce	-uce
furnace	accomplice	commerce	lettuce
menace	apprentice		
necklace	armistice	-ess	-os
palace	crevice	endless etc.	asbestos
preface	edifice	goddess etc.	chaos
solace	notice	madness etc.	thermos
surface	office	buttress	rhinoceros
terrace	jaundice	cypress	
	avarice	congress	-us
-as	malice	mattress	bonus
alias	cowardice	progress	calculus
bias	prejudice	prowess	octopus
canvas	justice	witness	stimulus
Christmas	service		terminus
pampas	practice (noun)		census
			fungus
	-ass	-is	syllabus
	compass	analysis	litmus
	cutlass	basis	nucleus
	harass (verb)	thesis	walrus
	trespass	Genesis	surplus
		hypothesis	ignoramus
		iris	opus
		clematis	radius
		oasis	rumpus
		pelvis	sinus
		synopsis	status
		arthritis etc.	focus
			minus
-ase	-ise	-ose	genius
carcase	practise (verb)	purpose	virus
purchase	promise		onus
	treatise		versus
			crocus

68

Common words in -ent and -ant, -ate, -ite, -ute

-able and -ible

This Latin-derived suffix denotes 'possibility'. Words with these endings which do *not* have such a connotation are:

constable	syllable	crucible
parable	vegetable	

-able is more common than *-ible*. Many of the words consist of a whole word + *-able*†. Anglo–Saxon words are found with this suffix added, and never with *-ible*, e.g. 'knowledgeable'. Some *-able* words which do not consist of a whole word + *-able*, have an 'a' in them which can be seen also in other words from the same root, e.g. 'applicable', c.f. 'application'.

-ible words which consist of a word + *-ible*† are rather uncommon. Some are listed in the third *-ible* column.

-ent / ənt /

Nouns	Adjectives
accident	absent
client	apparent
continent	confident
current	consistent
(water or	convenient
electr.)	different
gradient	eloquent
moment	eminent
opponent	evident
Orient	excellent
parent	frequent
resident	impudent
serpent	independent
student	insolent
talent	obedient
	permanent
	prominent
	silent
	violent

-ant / ənt /

Nouns	Adjectives
assailant	abundant
assistant	brilliant
consultant	defiant
contestant	distant
currant	dominant
(fruit)	fragrant
descendant	gallant
elephant	indignant
giant	instant
infant	luxuriant
informant	observant
inhabitant	pleasant
merchant	radiant
peasant	relevant
pheasant	
tenant	
truant	

-able

abominable	impeccable	palatable
administrable	indefatigable	portable
affable	indomitable	practicable
amiable	inevitable	separable
amicable	irreparable	sociable
applicable	laudable	tolerable
appreciable	manageable	vulnerable
despicable	miserable	(im)penetrable
(in)dispensable	navigable	(im)permeable
(in)explicable	negotiable	

-ite / ət /

definite	
exquisite	
favourite	
granite	
hypocrite	
infinite	
opposite	

-ate / ət /*

accurate	legitimate
appropriate	modulate
associate	moderate
certificate	intimate
climate	senate
curate	subordinate
delicate	syndicate
desolate	ultimate
duplicate	undergraduate
fortunate	separate
frigate	temperate
immediate	
inconsiderate	
intermediate	
intricate	

-ible

admissible	feasible	forcible
compatible	indelible	corruptible
comprehensible	invincible	digestible
credible	responsible	(ir)resistible
horrible	flexible	sensible
terrible	gullible	
legible	negligible	
intelligible	(in)fallible	
(im)possible	(in)edible)	
(in)audible	(in)tangible	
(in)visible	(im)perceptible	

-ute / ət /)

minute (noun)

* Some of these words, e.g. 'separate', 'moderate', are also verbs; in the verb, the 'a' in the final syllable is pronounced more clearly.

† For this purpose 'whole word' includes words ending in a *y* which changes to an *i*, e.g. 'verifiable' and words whose final *e* is dropped, e.g. 'describable'.

Noun endings

-or (some are also adjectives)	-our (mostly nouns)	-re (French) (mostly nouns)
anchor	labour	macabre
minor	arbour	sabre
major	harbour	fibre
junior	splendour	calibre
senior	odour	sombre
inferior	ardour	acre
superior	rigour	massacre
author	vigour	mediocre
tremor	behaviour	meagre
tenor	saviour	ogre
donor	valour	ochre
error	colour	sepulchre
terror	clamour	genre
mirror	glamour	theatre
horror	armour	spectre
juror	humour	metre etc.
solicitor	rumour	mitre
editor	tumour	centre
creditor	honour	lustre
suitor	vapour	manoeuvre
motor	contour	
ancestor	endeavour	
contributor	favour	Adjectives ending in -ar
tutor	savour	familiar
mayor	flavour	particular
surveyor	fervour	peculiar
governor		regular
sculptor	Nouns ending in -ar	polar
survivor	cellar	solar
visitor	burglar	similar
razor	sugar	vulgar
traitor	hangar	spectacular
possessor etc.	liar	perpendicular
administrator	pillar	circular
contractor etc.	caterpillar	popular
director etc.	dollar	singular
doctor etc.	collar	
conductor etc.		

-ary	-ery	-ory
1. Very common adjective ending	1. Adjective = having a certain character (-er + y)	1. -sory -tory adjectives — very common, especially -tory
necessary	papery	advisory
ordinary	peppery	compulsory
imaginary	powdery	cursory
stationary (not moving)	silvery	auditory
	thundery	satisfactory
	watery	contradictory
		preparatory etc.
	Note: fiery	
2. Limited number of nouns	2. Noun = 'stock in trade'	2. Limited number of nouns — -tory most common
adversary	grocery	theory
anniversary	cutlery	category
aviary	stationery	memory
boundary	cookery	history
burglary	jewellery etc.	directory
centenary		territory
diary	3. Noun = a locality	laboratory
dictionary	nursery	observatory
dispensary	shrubbery	lavatory
dromedary	vinery	repertory
estuary	rockery	rectory
January	Deanery etc.	dormitory
February		
glossary		
granary		
itinerary		
library		
mortuary		
salary		
sanctuary		
secretary		
summary		
vocabulary		
quandary		

-age		-iage	-ege
advantage	manage	carriage	college
average	message	marriage	privilege
baggage	mileage		
bandage	mortgage	-ige	
breakage	postage	vestige	
coinage	package		
cottage	passage		
(en)courage	plumage		
damage	ravage		
drainage	savage		
haulage	salvage		
homage	shortage		
hostage	village		
image			
luggage			

Other endings

-le	-el	-ey	-ie
table	parcel	donkey	calorie
uncle	angel	monkey	prairie
buckle	Rachel	turkey	sortie
ladle	satchel	(Turkey)	
trifle	camel	jersey	
gargle	panel	(Jersey)	
ample	barrel	guernsey	
title	petrel (bird)	(Guernsey)	
dazzle	easel	Anglesey	
	vessel	Bardsey	
BUT	novel	island	
model	towel	honey	
label	hazel	money	
rebel	cruel	barley	
chapel		parsley	
hostel		kidney	
		valley	
		trolley	
		pulley	
		jockey	
		hockey	
		chimney	
		abbey	

Note: The choice between -le and -el seems to depend on whether the preceding sound can easily be followed by /ˀl/ in speech without a vowel being interposed. It is useful to remember that soft c, g, must always be followed by -el, since the e has to be next to the c or g to soften it. The hard sounds of ck, k, hard g must be followed by -le, with the consonant l next to the g to make it hard.

The -le and -el lists are merely samples. They show how preceding consonants incline towards one or other ending.

-gue	-que	-k	-ine
fugue	cheque	yak	/ iːn /
league	plaque	flak	machine
plague	antique	kayak	sardine
rogue	unique	anorak	ravine
vogue	oblique	Slovak	margarine
prologue	clique	trek	plasticine
dialogue	technique	Bolshevik	routine
catalogue	physique		gabardine
fatigue	opaque		aubergine
intrigue	picturesque		iodine (and
	grotesque		other chemical
	statuesque		substances)
tongue	discotheque		
harangue	mosque		/ ən /
	brusque		engine
	Basque		imagine
	Baroque		genuine
			sanguine
			doctrine
			medicine
			discipline
			famine
			masculine
			feminine
			determine
			nectarine
			examine
			jasmine
			ermine
			heroine

2. Corruption of consonants

Dental and sibilant consonants at the end of a root tend to combine with a link vowel to form fricatives and affricatives.

Noun suffixes in -ti- -si- -ssi- -ci- -xi-

-ssion /ʃən/
In many cases the *ss* comes from a related verb or noun ending in -ss after a short vowel; such a doubling at the end occurs even in polysyllables when the stress is on the last syllable, e.g. 'express'. Naturally such -ssion words have short vowels. Sometimes, however, a root will alternate between *ss* and *tt*, and the verb will end in a single *t*, e.g. 'admit', 'admittance', 'admission'.

passion	confession	fission	discussion
	profession	admission	concussion
	session	submission	percussion
	procession	permission	repercussion
	succession	transmission	
	depression	commission	
	impression	omission	
	oppression		
	aggression		

-tion /ʃən/
This ending is very common after long vowels, but there are a number of *ition* words, and these are all short vowel.

Long-vowel words:

/eɪ/	/iː/	/əʊ/	/uː/
nation	completion	motion	solution
station	deletion	promotion	resolution
education	depletion	commotion	institution
examination		devotion	constitution
explanation		notion	restitution
imagination			retribution
admiration			attribution
exclamation			pollution
adoration			execution
exploration			diminution

Short-vowel words:

/æ/	/ɛ/	/ɪ/	/ɪ/
ration	discretion	condition	repetition
		addition	admonition
		position	exhibition
		composition	ambition
		exposition	ignition
		disposition	definition
		petition	prohibition
		competition	recognition

But note: fashion, cushion.
   Short vowel and consonant(s) also precede -*tion* ending, and the combination of sounds has to be carefully identified.

-tion /tʃən/
action	distinction	caption	question
fraction	compunction	exception	suggestion
satisfaction	junction	exemption	digestion
election		description	
selection		adoption	
protection		interruption	
perfection		corruption	
concoction			
suction			
construction			

Note: complexion, crucifixion.

-sion /ʒən/
When there is a vowel before this ending the sound /ʒ /rather than /ʃ / is produced by the *si* combination; consequently these words can be distinguished by sound. They usually have a long vowel before the ending except (as in the case of the -*tion* words) that an *i* is usually short, e.g.

evasion	cohesion	explosion	fusion
persuasion	adhesion	erosion	confusion
occasion			inclusion
invasion			conclusion
			profusion
			transfusion
			intrusion

/ɪ/

decision	revision
precision	provision
vision	television
division	

-sion /ʃən/

The only consonants found before this ending are *l*, *n*, *r*. Words ending in *-nsion* and *-rsion* are indistinguishable in sound from those ending in *-ntion* and *-rtion*, and can only be picked out by gradual familiarisation. However, there are no words ending in *-ltion*.

mention	*pens* ion	in *sert* ion	*vers* ion
in *tent* ion	sus *pens* ion	de *sert* ion	di *vers* ion
de *tent* ion	as *cens* ion	as *sert* ion	con *vers* ion
re *tent* ion	dis *sens* ion	exertion	a *vers* ion
at *tent* ion	ap *prehens* ion	(originally	ex *curs* ion
in *vent* ion	com *prehens* ion	ex-sert-	sub *mers* ion
pre *vent* ion	mansion	in Latin)	im *mers* ion
inter *vent* ion	ex *pans* ion	*port* ion	*tors* ion
	tens ion	ap *port* ion	
	ex *tens* ion	dis *tort* ion	
	di *mens* ion	ex *tort* ion	
		con *tort* ion	
		ab *ort* ion	

Comparing other words from the same root does not help to decide between *s* and *t*, because an original *-d* or *-t* ending may result in either *t* or *s*. Thus 'intend' and 'extend' contain the same root, but 'intend' gives 'intention' and 'extend' gives 'extension'!

However, it will be noticed that the first and fourth columns above have a number of words from the same root, and it will be easier to concentrate on these.

-cion, -cean

There are only two words ending in *-cion*:

> suspicion
> coercion

There is only one common word ending in *-cean*:

> ocean

There are also a few zoological and botanical terms, e.g. 'crustacean'.

-cian

The ending *-cian* generally indicates a person with a particular skill, and the *c* is already in the word for the skill concerned:

musician	politician
electrician	mathematician
technician	statistician
magician	

Adjective suffixes in -ti-, -si-, -ci-, -xi-, -ce-

-tious	-tial	-cious	-cial
ambitious	initial	tenacious	facial
cautious	spatial	spacious	beneficial
pretentious	substantial	gracious	superficial
infectious	circumstantial	voracious	racial
fictitious	residential	judicious	special
conscientious	presidential	officious	judicial
facetious	confidential	malicious	official
surreptitious	providential	delicious	artificial
superstitious	deferential	suspicious	financial
	torrential	auspicious	provincial
	essential	vicious	social
	potential	atrocious	commercial
	influential	conscious	
	partial	unconscious	
	credential		

-ceous	-xious	-sial
herbaceous	anxious	controversial
curvaceous	noxious	

Occasionally the existence of a *-tion* noun or a *t* in the stem strongly suggests *-ti-* rather than *-ci-*. However, some *-tious* and *-tial* adjectives come from nouns ending in *-ence* and *-ance*.

-tient	-(s)cient	-tience	-cience/y
patient	ancient	patience	conscience
quotient	deficient		deficiency
	proficient		proficiency
	efficient		efficiency
	sufficient		sufficiency
	prescient		

-tual

    actual
    factual
    mutual
    punctual

Some of these are frequently pronounced with a /tʃ/ sound, but this is not universal.

-dure, -dual

    procedure
    gradual

These are frequently pronounced with a /dʒ/ sound, but this is not universal. In 'endure' the emphasis on the root prevents such corruption.

-gu-

Although this is not, of course, dental or sibilant, it is frequently pronounced /gw/ in this position.

    penguin
    languid
    language
    anguish
    distinguish
    sanguine

3. Link vowels — *i* and *e*

Link vowels *i* or *e* between a root syllable and a suffix beginning with a vowel, even if not merged with a previous consonant, lose their distinctive quality and cannot be distinguished by sound; the sound is sometimes almost a consonantal *y*; *i* is more usual than *e* as a link vowel.

radio	material	idiot	Canadian
radiator	serial	chariot	Indian
gladiator	secretarial	patriot	Italian
radiant	trivial	appropriate	Spaniard
brilliant	aerial	immediate	insignia
valiant	cordial	retaliate	bacteria
convenient	genial	audience	ammonia
ingredient	obvious	experience	malaria
obedient	dubious	convenience	
gradient	studious	onion	
familiar	devious	union	
peculiar	serious	champion	
junior	furious	companion	
senior	various	million	
interior	glorious	medallion	
exterior	tedious	rebellion	
inferior	notorious	dominion	
superior	precarious	battalion	
warrior	victorious	pavilion	
barrier	punctilious		
frontier	industrious		
	ingenious		

Note: *di* in 'Indian' is often pronounced /dʒ/ . In 'carriage', 'marriage', 'parliament' the *i* is not heard at all.

An *e* link vowel is not very common. Occasionally the *e* can be detected in related words, but there is not often such help available.

miscreant	instantaneous	plenteous
linear ('line')	simultaneous	piteous
cereal ('Ceres')	(simultaneity)	homogeneous
ethereal	spontaneous	(homogeneity)
funereal	(spontaneity)	
chameleon	courteous	
galleon	erroneous	
	hideous	
	miscellaneous	

Note: *de* in 'hideous' is often pronounced /dʒ/ .

With a *g* preceding it, the vowel, whether *e* or *i*, is not heard at all, but is nevertheless indispensable to soften the *g* before *a* or *o*.

region	pigeon	pageant
legion	dungeon	sergeant (/sadʒ–/)
religion	surgeon	
religious	bludgeon	
contagion	gorgeous	
contagious	courageous	
prodigious		
prestigious		
sacrilegious		
(/–lɪdʒəs/)		

Note: soldier, truncheon, luncheon (perhaps archaic).

Section 11

Spare Parts

Functions of an *e*

The letter e has a normal function as a full vowel, which can be long or short, and also as a vowel which combines with other vowels to make vowel digraphs, and with *r, w, y*

However, besides these it also performs various other useful functions as a sort of 'spare part'.

1. It lengthens an earlier vowel, with a consonant or occasionally two intervening, e.g.

fate	compete	ride	hope	tune
ache		blithe	clothes	
haste				
		type		
		scythe		

2. It softens an immediately preceding *c*, or *g* (as also do *i* and *y*), e.g.

cell	prince	sledge

Note that *ge* is the only possible spelling for that sound in English at the end of a word. Foreign words sometimes end in *j*, e.g. 'raj'.

3. It forms an ending with *v, s,* and *z*. In English *v* and *z* are never found without *e* at the end of a word unless doubled, although a foreign word may be, e.g. 'fez', or an abbreviation, e.g. 'rev'. *s* on its own is normally reserved for plural endings and third person singular endings, e.g. 'hits'.

have	breeze	house
give		noise

In none of these words is the *e* lengthening the vowel.

4. It forms a vowel digraph at the end of a word, with *o, u, i* and *y*. Although not strictly necessary to make the sound, it often enables the word to be three letters rather than two, more usual for verbs and nouns in English, e.g.

hoe	sue	tie	dye
			eye

5. It intervenes between a final single vowel, usually found with foreign words rather than English ones, and the *s* plural ending (see p., 45), and between *sh, ss, ch, x* and the *s* plural ending to make the word pronounceable.

Functions of an apostrophe

An apostrophe performs a similar 'spare part' function:

1. It replaces a missing letter, e.g. 'don't'.
2. It denotes possession, when used after a noun, e.g. 'people's'.
3. It intervenes between a letter name or arabic number and the *s* plural, e.g. 'c's', '4's'.

Dropping an *e*

When suffixing, one has to consider whether a final *e*, in cases 1–4 above, is any longer needed to perform the function that it has been performing.

1. If it is lengthening a previous vowel, and the suffix begins with a vowel, a single consonant (or consonant digraph) between two vowels will ensure that the previous vowel remains long; the *e* is therefore not needed and can be dropped, e.g.

hate	hating	bathe	bathing
hope	hoped	ache	aching
type	typist		
ride	ridable		

Sometimes, even two consonants, if closely linked, preserve the long vowel, e.g. change, changing.

However, if the suffix begins with a consonant, the *e* will still be needed if the previous vowel is to stay long, e.g. excite excitement (contrast 'fitment').

There are one or two exceptions, but these seem understandable:

'wholly'   It would be very difficult to say 'wholely', and -oll is in any case regularly pronounced with a long vowel, e.g. 'roll'.

'holey'   Keeping the e distinguishes it from 'holy' (sacred).

'ninth'   If the e were kept it would give the appearance of two syllables with the suffix -eth, as in 'cometh'.

'mileage'   This is more common than 'milage', keeping the full word for the unit, as in 'yardage', 'footage'.

2. The c or g will remain soft if the suffix begins with e, i or y, but not if the suffix begins with a, o or u. In these last cases, therefore, the e needs to be retained, e.g.

place	placing	replaceable	placement
manage	managing	manageable	management

There is an exception, again understandable:

'singeing'   This distinguishes it from 'singing'. Note that other ng words drop the e, e.g. 'fringing', 'hinging', 'sponging'.

'ageing'   (keeping the whole original word) is more usual, but 'aging' is found.

3. The e after a v or z is not considered necessary if the suffix begins with a vowel, but these letters are not normally followed by consonants in English; se seems to follow the same pattern, even with less justification perhaps, e.g.

living	involvement
breezing	breezeless
housing	endorsement

4. The words are few in number and there seems no general rule.
-ie and -ue words tend to drop the e before vowels, with i turning to y, e.g.

rue	ruing	tie	tying
sue	suing	die	dying
ensue	ensuing	lie	lying
pursue	pursuing		

-ye words tend to keep the e, e.g.

dye   dyeing (which distinguishes it from 'dying' (perishing)

eye   eyeing — usually (without the e one might be unsure over pronunciation)

-oe words keep the e

hoe	hoeing
toe	toeing
shoe	shoeing
canoe	canoeing

However, these last words are a hotchpotch collection. In several the e is a relic of a different original letter and therefore perhaps more likely to be retained (e.g. 'canoe' < Spanish 'canoa').

Doubling and non-doubling of consonants

ck, tch, dge in polysyllabic words

ck: This ending is not common at the end of a polysyllabic word; the Greek-derived suffix -ic is a very frequent ending. However, when a suffix beginning with a vowel is added to this, ck is used to preserve the hard sound, e.g.

trafficker	trafficking	trafficked
picnicker	picnicking	picnicked

There are, however, a few two-syllable words ending in ck. These are often words made up of two single-syllable words, as in the first column:

padlock	hammock
knapsack	paddock
haversack	mattock
rucksack	bullock
ransack	hassock
haystack	buttocks
hunchback	barrack
homesick	derrick
woodchuck	limerick
	rollick

tch: This is also not commonly found at the end of polysyllabic words unless they are composed of two single-syllable words, as in the first column:

hopscotch	dispatch
hotchpotch	bewitch
nuthatch	

Note, however 'attach' 'detach' (which have the same French root).

dge: This is likewise not a common ending in polysyllabic words (-*ge*, e.g. -*age*, is very frequent). Polysyllables ending in -*dge* are frequently compounds of the single-syllable *dge* verbs 'bridge', 'lodge', 'judge', 'grudge', e.g. 'abridge', 'dislodge', 'adjudge', 'begrudge'. There are only a few others:

porridge
cartridge
partridge
selvedge
knowledge (acknowledge)

Words which do not double after short vowels

The words which do not double consonants after short vowels tend to be:

1. Words of Greek origin. Greek was a language containing many single consonants and single vowels, many of them short, with no heavy stresses; it has given much scientific and technical vocabulary to English. -*ic* and -*ology* are particularly common endings derived from Greek. The following are all words derived from Greek:

clinic	conic	topology	camel	sandal
topic	erotic	analogy	panel	
manic	exotic	philology		
tonic	idiotic	chronology	clematis	
colic	automatic	apology	analysis	
cynic	atomic		synthesis	
lyric			Genesis	
sonic				

2. Words of French and originally Latin derivation which did not have a double consonant in those languages and which still retain approximately their French form.

city	talon	manage	robin
pity	melon	damage	satin
infinity	lemon	garage	cabin
facility	crayon	visage	Latin
hostility	dragon	forage	cretin
minority	baton	borage	rosin
severity	comparison	homage	toxin
disparity	dominion	image	Matins
clarity			
verity	palace	petal	finish
	menace	metal	perish
modify		pedal	polish
	limit	moral	abolish
civil	habit		astonish
peril	credit	tepid	blemish
vigil	profit	solid	diminish
basil	spirit	stolid	
cavil	exhibit	rapid	
devil	deposit	valid	
		rabid	
		rigid	
		arid	
		avid	

Although many words with these particular endings do not double, a few do, e.g. 'rabbit', 'horrid'.

Note that *v* never doubles, e.g. 'ever', 'never', 'every', 'river'. Note also 'very', 'bury', 'widow'.

Appendix II

Books and Materials List

Cotterell Checklist by Gill Cotterell. Wisbech, Cambs: LDA.

Phonic Reference Cards by Gill Cotterell. Wisbech, Cambs: LDA.

Remedial Spelling by Violet Brand. Baldock, Herts: Egon Publishers (1985).

Help for the Dyslexic Adolescent by E. G. Stirling, obtainable from the author (1986).

Which is Which by E.G. Stirling, obtainable as above (1990).

A Spelling Checklist for Dyslexics by E.G. Stirling, obtainable as above (1984).

Dyslexia at College by T.R. Miles and D.E. Gilroy. London: Routledge (1986).

The Spell of Words by Elsie T. Rak. Cambridge, Mass: Educators Publishing Service Inc. (1980).

Spellbound by Elsie T. Rak. Cambridge, Mass: Educators Publishing service Inc. (1981).

Solving Language Difficulties by Amey Steere, Caroline Z. Peck and Linda Kahn. Cambridge, Mass: Educators Publishing Service Inc., Rev. Ed. (1971).

Unscrambling Spelling by C. Klein and R.R. Millar. Sevenoaks: Hodder and Stoughton (1990).

Word Quest by Michael Thomson. Wisbech, Cambs: LDA (1986).

ACE — Aurally Coded English Spelling Dictionary by David Moseley and Catherine Nicol (6th edn, 1990).

Pergamon Dictionary of Perfect Spelling by Christine Maxwell. Leeds: Arnold (1977).

See also Study skills book list, p. 47.

International Phonetic Alphabet Symbols for Transcribing Sounds of English Letters or Groups of Letters

Consonant sounds

b k or s d f g or dʒ h dʒ k l
m n p kw r s or z t v w ks j z

Consonant digraphs

θ (th as in 'thin') ð (th as in 'this') ʃ (sh) tʃ (ch)
hw (wh if pronounced other than /w/)

Short vowels

æ ɛ ɪ ɒ ʌ

Schwa

ə

Long vowels

eɪ iː aɪ əʊ uː or juː

Other vowel digraphs

ʊ	'oo' as in 'good'
uː	'oo' as in 'moon'
ʊə	'oy' 'oi'
ɑː	'ar' (if *r* not pronounced)
ɔː	'or' (if *r* not pronounced)
ɜː	'er' 'ir' 'ur' (if *r* not pronounced)
ɪə	'ear' 'eer' 'ier' (if *r* not pronounced)
ʊə	'oor' as in 'moor'* (if *r* not pronounced)
aɪə	'ire' 'yre' (if *r* not pronounced)
aʊ	'ow' as in 'cow' 'ou' as in 'out'

* In some areas all such words are pronounced like 'door'.

Other English sound combinations

ˀl	=	*-le -el* ending
ˀn	=	*-en -un -an*, e.g. in 'fatten' 'button' 'tartan'
ŋ	=	*-ng*
ʒ	=	*-si- -su-* in 'television' 'treasure'
x	=	*ch* in Welsh or Scottish words

Index